Buddhist Parab

ISBN: 978 1 8647617 2 6

AXIOM
AUSTRALIA

www.axiompublishing.com.au

Printed in Malaysia

Buddhist Parables

tales to illuminate

Content

I AM AWAKE

When the Buddha started to wander around India shortly after his enlightenment, he encountered several men who recognised him to be a very extraordinary being.

They asked him, "Are you a god?"

"No," he replied.

"Are you a reincarnation of god?"

"No," he replied.

"Are you a wizard, then?"

"No."

"Well, are you a man?"

"No."

"So what are you?" they asked, being very perplexed.

"I am awake."

Buddha means "The Awakened One". How to awaken is all he taught.

RELYING ON JOY

At the time of Buddha, there lived an old beggar woman called 'Relying on Joy'. She used to watch the kings, princes, and people making offerings to Buddha and his disciples, and there was nothing she would have liked more than to be able to do the same. So she went out begging, but at the end of a whole day all she had was one small coin. She took it to the oil-merchant to try to buy some oil. He told her that she could not possibly buy anything with so little. But when he heard that she wanted it to make an offering to Buddha, he took pity on her and gave her the oil she wanted. She took it to the monastery, where she lit a lamp. She placed it before Buddha, and made this wish: "I have nothing to offer but this tiny lamp. But through this offering, in the future may I be blessed with the lamp of wisdom. May I free all beings from their darkness. May I purify all their obstructions, and lead them to enlightenment." That night the oil in all the other lamps went out. But the beggar woman's lamp was still burning at dawn, when Buddha's disciple Maudgalyayana came to collect all the lamps.

When he saw that one was still alight, full of oil and with a new wick, he thought, "There's no reason why this lamp should still be burning in the day time," and he tried to blow it out. But it kept on burning. He tried to snuff it out with his fingers, but it stayed alight. He tried to smother it with his robe, but still it burned on. The Buddha had watched all along, and said, "Maudgalyayana, do you want to put out that lamp? You cannot. You cannot even move it, let alone put it out. If you were to pour the water from all oceans over this lamp, it still wouldn't go out.

The water in all the rivers and the lakes of the world could not extinguish it. Why not? Because this lamp was offered with devotion and with purity of heart and mind. And that motivation has made it of tremendous benefit." When Buddha had said this, the beggar woman approached him, and he made a prophesy that in the future she would become a perfect buddha, called 'Light of the Lamp.' So it is our motivation, good or bad, that determines the fruit of our actions.

LYING

This was said by the Lord...

"Bhikkhus, I say that for an individual who transgresses in one thing, there is no evil deed whatsoever he would not do. What is that one thing? It is this, bhikkhus: deliberately telling a lie."

There is no evil that cannot be done
By a person who deliberately lies,
Who transgresses in one thing,
Taking no account of the next world.

RELEASING THE COWS

One day the Buddha was sitting in the wood with thirty or forty monks. They had an excellent lunch and they were enjoying the company of each other. There was a farmer passing by and the farmer was very unhappy. He asked the Buddha and the monks whether they had seen his cows passing by. The Buddha said they had not seen any cows passing by.

The farmer said, "Monks, I'm so unhappy. I have twelve cows and I don't know why they all ran away. I have also a few acres of a sesame seed plantation and the insects have eaten up everything. I suffer so much I think I am going to kill myself.

The Buddha said, "My friend, we have not seen any cows passing by here. You might like to look for them in the other direction." So the farmer thanked him and ran away, and the Buddha turned to his monks and said, "My dear friends, you are the happiest people in the world. You don't have any cows to lose. If you have too many cows to take care of, you will be very busy.

"That is why, in order to be happy, you have to learn the art of cow releasing. You release the cows one by one. In the beginning you thought that those cows were essential to your happiness, and you tried to get more and more cows. But now you realise that cows are not really conditions for your happiness; they constitute an obstacle for your happiness. That is why you are determined to release your cows."

ASANGA

Asanga was one of the most famous Indian Buddhist saints, and lived in the fourth century. He went to the mountains to do a solitary retreat, concentrating all his meditation practice on the Buddha Maitreya, in the fervent hope that he would be blessed with a vision of this Buddha and receive teachings from him.

For six years Asanga meditated in extreme hardship, but did not even have one auspicious dream. He was disheartened and thought he would never succeed with his aspiration to meet the Buddha Maitreya, and so he abandoned his retreat and left his hermitage. He had not gone far down the road when he saw a man rubbing an enormous iron bar with a strip of silk. Asanga went up to him and asked him what he was doing. "I haven't got a needle," the man replied, "so I'm going to make one out of this iron bar." Asanga stared at him, astounded; even if the man were able to manage it in a hundred years, he thought, what would be the point? He said to himself:
"Look at the trouble people give themselves over things that are totally absurd. You are doing something really valuable, spiritual practice, and you're not nearly so dedicated." He turned around and went back to his retreat. Another three years went by, still without the slightest sign from the Buddha Maitreya. "Now I know for certain," he thought "I'm never going to succeed." So he left again, and soon came to a bend in the road where there was a huge rock, so tall it seemed to touch the sky. At the foot of the rock was a man busily rubbing it with a feather soaked in water. "What are you doing?" Asanga asked. "This rock is so big it's stopping the sun from shining on my house, so I'm

trying to get rid of it." Asanga was amazed at the man's indefatigable energy, and ashamed at his own lack of dedication. He returned to his retreat.

Three more years passed, and still he had not even had a single good dream. He decided, once and for all, that it was hopeless, and he left his retreat for good. The day wore on, and in the afternoon he came across a dog lying by the side of the road. It had only its front legs, and the whole of the lower part of its body was rotting and covered with maggots. Despite its pitiful condition, the dog was snapping at passers-by and pathetically trying to bite them by dragging itself along the ground with its two good legs.

Asanga was overwhelmed with a vivid and unbearable feeling of compassion. He cut a piece of flesh off his own body and gave it to the dog to eat. Then he bent down to take off the maggots that were consuming the dog's body. But he suddenly thought he might hurt them if he tried to pull them out with his fingers, and realised that the only way to remove them would be on his tongue. Asanga knelt on the ground, and looking at the horrible festering, writhing mass, closed his eyes. He leant closer and put out his tongue. The next thing he knew, his tongue was touching the ground. He opened his eyes and looked up. The dog was gone; there in its place was the Buddha Maitreya, ringed by a shimmering aura of light. "At last," said Asanga, "why did you never appear to me before?"

Maitreya spoke softly: "It is not true that I have never appeared to you before. I was with you all the time, but your negative karma and obscurations prevented you from seeing me. Your twelve years of practice dissolved them slightly so that you were at last able to see the dog. Then, thanks to your genuine and heartfelt compassion, all those obscurations were completely swept away and you can see me before you with your very own eyes. If you don't believe that this is what happened, put me on your shoulder and try and see if anyone else can see me." Asanga put Maitreya on his right shoulder and went to the marketplace, where he began to ask everyone: "What have I got on my shoulder?" "Nothing," most people said, and hurried on. Only one old woman, whose karma had been slightly purified, answered: "You've got the rotting corpse of an old dog on your shoulder, that's all." Asanga at last understood the boundless power of compassion that had purified and transformed his karma, and so made him a vessel fit to receive the vision and instruction of Maitreya. Then the Buddha Maitreya, whose name means "loving kindness," took Asanga to a heavenly realm, and there gave him many sublime teachings that are among the most important in the whole of Buddhism.

HELL

The Buddha, in one of his former lives, was in Hell. Before he became a Buddha he had suffered a lot in many lives. He made a lot of mistakes, like all of us. He made himself suffer, and he made people around him suffer. Sometimes he made very big mistakes, and that is why in one of his previous lives he was in Hell.

The Buddha was in Hell because he had done something wrong, extremely wrong, that caused a lot of suffering to himself and to others. That is why he found himself in Hell. In that life of his, he hit the bottom of suffering, because that Hell was the worst of all Hells. With him there was another man, and together they had to work very hard, under the direction of a soldier who was in charge of Hell. It was dark, it was cold, and at the same time it was very hot. The guard did not seem to have a heart. It did not seem that he knew anything about suffering. He did not know anything about the feelings of other people, so he just beat up the two men in Hell. He was in charge of the two men, and his task was to make them suffer as much as possible.

That guard also suffered a lot. It looked like he didn't have any compassion within him. It looked like he didn't have any love in his heart. It looked like he did not have a heart. He behaved like a robber. When looking at him, when listening to him, it did not seem that one could contact a human being, because he was so brutal. He was not sensitive to people's suffering and pain. That is why he was beating the two men in Hell, and making them suffer a lot. And the Buddha was one of these two men in one of his previous lives.

The guard had an instrument with three iron points, and every time he wanted the two men to go ahead, he used this to push them on the back, and of course blood came out of their backs. He did not allow them to relax; he was always pushing and pushing and pushing. He himself also looked like he was being pushed by something behind him. Have you ever felt that kind of pushing behind your back? Even if there was no one behind you, you have felt that you were being pushed and pushed to do things you don't like to do, and to say the things you don't like to say, and in doing that you created a lot of suffering for yourself and the people around you. Maybe there is something behind us that is pushing and pushing. Sometimes we say horrible things, and do horrible things, that we did not want to say or do, yet we were pushed by something from behind. So we said it, and we did it, even if we didn't want to do it. That was what happened to the guard in Hell: he tried to push, because he was being pushed. He caused a lot of damage to the two men. The two men were very cold, very hungry, and he was always pushing and beating them and causing them a lot of problems.

One afternoon, the man who was the Buddha in a former life saw the guard treating his companion so brutally that something in him rose up. Deep within the Buddha was a pressure coming up, and he wanted to intervene, even knowing perfectly well that if he did, he would be beaten by the guard. That impulse was very strong in him, and he could not stand it anymore. He turned around, and he faced the guard without any heart, and said, "Why don't you leave him alone for a moment? Why do you keep beating him and pushing him like that? Don't you have a heart?"

That was what he said, this man who was to be the Buddha. When the guard saw him protesting like that, and heard him, he was very angry, and he used his fork, and he planted it right in the chest of the Buddha. As a result, the Buddha died right away, and he was reborn the very same minute into the body of a human being. He escaped Hell, and became a human being living on earth, just because compassion was born in him, strong enough for him to have the courage to intervene to help his fellow man in Hell.

The other fellow saw the Buddha die. He was angry, and for the first time he was touched by compassion: the other person must have had some love, some compassion to have the courage to intervene for his sake.

That gave rise to some compassion in him also. He looked at the guard, and he said, "My friend was right, you don't have a heart. You can only create suffering for yourself and for other people. I don't think that you are a happy person. You have killed him." And after he said that, the guard was also very angry at him, and he used his fork, and planted the fork in the stomach of the second man, who also died right away, and was reborn as a human being on earth.

Both of them escaped Hell, and had a chance to begin anew on earth, as full human beings. What happened to the guard, the one who had no heart? He felt very lonely, because in that Hell there were only three people and now the other two were dead. He began to see that these two were not very kind, or very nice, but to have people living with us is a wonderful thing. Now the two other people were dead, and he was alone, utterly alone there.

He could not bear that kind of loneliness, and Hell became very difficult for him. Out of that suffering he learned something: he learned that you cannot live alone. Man is not our enemy. You cannot hate man, you cannot kill man, you cannot reduce man to nothingness, because if you kill man, with whom will you live? He made a vow that if he had to take care of other people in Hell, he would learn how to deal with them in a nicer way, and a transformation took place in his heart. In fact, To believe that he did not have a heart is wrong—everyone has a heart. We need something or someone to touch that heart, to transform it into a human heart. So this time the feeling of loneliness, the desire to be with other humans, was born in him. That is why he decided that if he had to guard other people in Hell, he would know how to deal with them with more compassion. At that time, the door of Hell opened, and a bodhisattva appeared, with all the radiance of a bodhisattva. The bodhisattva said, "Goodness has been born in you, so you don't have to endure Hell very long. You will die quickly and be reborn as a human very soon."

EAT WHEN YOU'RE HUNGRY

Someone asked a Zen Master, "How do you practice Zen?"

The master said, "When you are hungry, eat; when you are tired, sleep."

"Isn't that what everyone does anyway?"

The master replied, "No, No. Most people entertain a thousand desires when they eat and scheme over a thousand plans when they sleep."

KARMA (THE FOUR WIVES)

Once there was a man who had four wives. According to the social system and circumstances of ancient India, it was possible for a man to have several wives. The Indian had become ill and was about to die. At the end of his life, he felt very lonely and so asked the first wife to accompany him to the other world.

'My dear wife,' he said, 'I loved you day and night, I took care of you throughout my whole life. Now I am about to die, will you please go with me wherever I go after my death?'

He expected her to answer yes. But she answered, 'My dear husband, I know you always loved me. And you are going to die. Now it is time to separate from you. Goodbye, my dear.'

He called his second wife to his sickbed and begged her to follow him in death. He said, 'My dear second wife, you know how I loved you. Sometimes I was afraid you might leave me, but I held on to you strongly. My dear, please come with me.'

The second wife expressed herself rather coldly. 'Dear husband, your first wife refused to accompany you after your death. How can I follow you? You loved me only for your own selfish sake.'

Lying in his deathbed, he called his third wife, and asked her to follow him. The third wife replied, with tears in her eyes, 'My dear, I pity you and I feel sad for myself. Therefore I shall accompany you to the graveyard. This is my last duty to you.' The third wife thus also refused to follow him to death.

Three wives had refused to follow him after his death. Now he recalled that there was another wife, his fourth wife, for whom he didn't care very much. He had treated her like a slave and had always showed much displeasure with her. He now thought that if he asked her to follow him to death, she certainly would say no.

But his loneliness and fear were so severe that he made the effort to ask her to accompany him to the other world. The fourth wife gladly accepted her husband's request.

'My dear husband,' she said, 'I will go with you. Whatever happens, I am determined to be with you forever. I cannot be separated from you."

This is the story of 'A Man and His Four Wives.' Gautama Buddha concluded the story as follows:

'Every man and woman has four wives or husbands. What do these wives signify?'

THE FIRST WIFE

The first 'wife' is our body. We love our body day and night. In the morning, we wash our face, put on clothing and shoes. We give food to our body. We take care of our body like the first wife in this story. But unfortunately, at the end of our life, the body, the first 'wife' cannot follow us to the next world. As it is stated in a commentary, 'When the last breath leaves our body, the healthy colour of the face is transformed, and we lose the appearance of radiant life. Our loved ones may gather around and lament, but to no avail. When such an event occurs, the body is sent into an open field and cremated, leaving only the white ashes.' This is the destination of our body.

THE SECOND WIFE

The second 'wife' stands for our fortune, our material things, money, property, fame, position, and job that we worked hard to attain. We are attached to these material possessions. We are afraid to lose these material things and wish to possess much more. There is no limit. At the end of our life these things cannot follow us to death. Whatever fortune we have piled up, we must leave it. We came into this world with empty hands. During our life in this world, we have the illusion that we obtained a fortune. At death, our hands are empty. We can't hold our fortune after our death, just as the second wife told her husband: 'You hold me with your ego-centred selfishness. Now it is time to say goodbye.'

THE THIRD WIFE

This is the relationship of our parents, sister and brother, all relatives, friends, and society. They will go as far as the graveyard, with tears in their eyes. They are sympathetic and saddened.

Thus, we cannot depend on our physical body, our fortune, and our society. We are born alone and we die alone. No one will accompany us after our death.

THE FOURTH WIFE

The fourth 'wife' is our mind. When we deeply observe and recognise that our minds are filled with anger, greed, and dissatisfaction, we are having a good look at our lives. The anger, greed, and dissatisfaction are karma, the law of causation. We cannot be separated from our own karma. As the fourth wife told her dying husband, 'I will follow you wherever you go.'

ANGULIMALA
A Story of the Power of Compassion

There was once the son of a Brahmin (the highest 'priestly' caste in India) in the court of King Pasenadi of Kosala, whose name was Ahimsaka. He was sent to Taxila for his studies. Ahimsaka was intelligent and obedient to this teacher; therefore he was liked by both the teacher and his wife. This made the other pupils jealous of him. So they went to the teacher and falsely accused Ahimsaka of having an immoral relationship with the teacher's wife. At first, he did not believe them, but after hearing it a number of times, he thought it was true and vowed to have revenge on Ahimsaka. He thought that to kill him would reflect badly on him. His rage prompted him to suggest the unthinkable to the young and innocent Ahimsaka. He told his pupil to kill a thousand human beings and to bring the right thumb of each as payment for teaching him. Of course the youngster would not even think of such a thing, so he was banished from the teacher's house and returned to his parents.

When his father learned why Ahimsaka had been expelled, he became furious with his son, and would hear no reason. On that very day, with the rain pouring down, he ordered Ahimsaka to leave the house. Ahimsaka went to his mother and asked her advice, but she could not go against the will of her husband. Next Ahimsaka went to the house of his betrothed (in accord with the ancient custom in India calling for betrothal of children long before their actual marriage), but when the family learned why Ahimsaka had been turned out of school, they drove him off. The shame, anger, fear, and despair of Ahimsaka drove him out of his mind. His suffering mind could only recollect the teacher's order: to collect 1,000 human thumbs. And so he started killing, and as he killed, the thumbs he collected were hung on a tree, but as they were destroyed by crows and vultures, he later wore a garland of the fingers to keep track of the number.

Because of this he came to be known as Angulimala (finger garland) and became the terror of the countryside. The king himself heard about the exploits of Angulimala, and he decided to capture him. When Mantani, Ahimsaka's mother, heard about the king's intention, she went to the forest in a desperate bid to save her son. By this time, the chain around the neck of Angulimala had 999 fingers in it, just one finger short of 1,000.

The Buddha; learned of the mother's attempt to dissuade her son from, and reflected that if he did not intervene, Angulimala, who was on the lookout for the last person to make up the 1,000, would see his mother and might kill her. In that case, he would have to suffer an even longer period for his evil karma. Out of compassion, the Buddha left for the forest.

Angulimala, after many sleepless days and nights, was very tired and near exhaustion. At the same time, he was very anxious to kill the last person to make up his full quota of 1,000 and so complete his task. He made up his mind to kill the first person he met. As he looked down from his mountain perch, he saw a woman on the road below. He wanted to fulfil his vow to complete the 1,000 thumbs, but as he approached, he saw it was his mother. At the same time, the Buddha was approaching, and Angulimala had just enough presence of mind to decide to kill the wandering monk instead of his mother. He set out after the Blessed

One with his knife raised. But the Buddha kept moving ahead of him. Angulimala just could not catch up with him. Finally, he cried out, "O Bhikkhu, stop, stop!" And the Enlightened One replied, "I have stopped. It is you who have not stopped." Angulimala did not catch the significance of these words, so he asked, "O bhikkhu! Why do you say that you have stopped while I have not?"

The Buddha replied, "I say that I have stopped because I have given up killing all beings. I have given up ill-treating all beings, and have established myself in universal love, patience, and knowledge through reflection. But you have not given up killing or ill treating others and you are not yet established in universal love and patience. Hence, you are the one who has not stopped." On hearing these words Angulimala was recalled to reality, and thought, these are the words of a wise man. This monk is so very wise and so very brave that he must be the leader of the monks. Indeed, he must be the Enlightened One himself! He must have come here specially to make me see the light. So thinking, he threw away his weapons and asked the Blessed One to admit to the Order of the bhikkhus, which the Buddha did.

When the king and his men came to capture Angulimala, they found him at the monastery of the Buddha. Finding that Angulimala had given up his evil ways and become a bhikkhu, the king and his men agreed to leave him alone. During his stay at the monastery, Angulimala ardently practiced meditation.

Angulimala had no peace of mind because even in his solitary meditation he used to recall memories of his past and the pathetic cries of his unfortunate victims. As a result of his evil karma, while seeking alms in the streets he would become a target of stray stones and sticks and he would return to the Jetavana monastery with broken head and blood flowing, cut and bruised, to be reminded by the Buddha: "My son Angulimala. You have done away with evil. Have patience. This is the effect of the evil deeds you have committed in the existence. Your evil karma would have made you suffer through innumerable existences had I not met you."

One morning while going on an almsround in Savatthi, Angulimala heard someone crying out in pain. When he came to know that a pregnant lady was having labour pains and facing difficulty to deliver the child, he reflected, all worldly beings are subject to suffering. Moved by compassion, he reported the suffering of this poor woman to the Buddha who advised him to recite the following words of truth, which later came to be known as Angulimala Paritta. Going to the presence of the suffering woman, he sat on a seat separated from her by a screen, and uttered these words:

Sister, since the day I became an arahat
I have not consciously destroyed
The life of any living beings.
By this truth, may you be well
And may your unborn child be well.

Instantly the woman delivered her child with ease. Both the mother and chid were well and healthy. Even today many resort to this paritta.

Angulimala liked living in solitude and in seclusion. Later he passed away peacefully. As an arahat, he attained parinibbana.

Other bhikkhus asked the Buddha where Angulimala was reborn, and when the Blessed One replied, my son Angulimala has attained parinibbana, they could hardly believe it. So they asked whether it was possible that such a man who had in fact killed so many people could have attained parinibbana. To this question, the Buddha replied, "Bhikkhus, Angulimala had done much evil because he did not have good friends. But later, he found good friends and with their help and good advice he became steadfast and mindful in practicing the dhamma and meditation. Thus, his evil deeds have been overwhelmed by good karma and his mind has been completely rid of all defilements."

The Buddha said of Angulimala

"Whose evil deed is obscured by good,
he illumines this world like the
moon freed from a cloud."

The power of love and compassion are stronger than any evil, and are absolute conditions for awakening.

EASIER KNOWN THAN DONE

One day, the famous poet Bai Ju-Yi (Po Chu-I) asked Master Niao-Wo, "What is the essence of the Buddha's teaching?"

Master Niao-Wo said, "Refrain from all unwholesome deeds and perform all wholesome deeds."

Bai chuckled, "Ha! Even a child knows that."

The master replied, "A child may know it, but not even a one-hundred-year-old can do it."

THE BABY'S FLESH

A young couple and their two-year-old child were trying to cross the desert, and they ran out of food. After deep reflection, they realised that in order to survive they had to kill their son and eat his flesh. They calculated that if they ate such and such a proportion of their baby's flesh and carried the rest on their shoulder to dry, it would last the rest of their journey. But with every morsel of their baby's flesh they ate, the young couple cried and cried. After he told this story, the Buddha asked, "Dear friends, do you think the young couple enjoyed eating their son's flesh?"

"No, Lord, it would not be possible for them to enjoy eating their son's flesh." The Buddha said, "Yet many people eat the flesh of their parents, their children, and their grandchildren and do not know it."

PICNIC/MEDITATION

In answer to the observation that some people say they do not meditate because they are too busy, the Dalai Lama told the following story:

A monk keeps promising his student that he will take him on a picnic but is always too busy to do so. One day they see a procession carrying a corpse.

"Where is he going?" the monk asks his student.

"On a picnic."

FATE IS IN YOUR OWN HANDS

Once upon a time, there was a general who was leading his army into battle against an enemy ten times the size of his own.

Along the way to the battle field, the troops stopped by a small temple to pray for victory. The general held up a coin and told his troops, "I am going to implore the gods to help us crush our enemy. If this coin lands with the heads on top, we'll win. If it's tails, we'll lose. Our fate is in the hands of the gods. Let's pray wholeheartedly."

After a short prayer, the general tossed the coin. It landed with the heads on top. The troops were overjoyed and went into the battle with high spirit. Just as predicted, the smaller army won the battle.

The soldiers were exalted, "It's good to have the gods on our side! No one can change what they have determined."

"Really?" The general showed them the coin—both sides of it were heads.

NOBODY TOLD ME ANYTHING

A disciple asked his Dharma Master: "How can I calm my mind?" The master said, "I am too busy to talk to you right now. Why not consult your First Dharma Brother?"

He did as he was told and asked the same question. The First Dharma Brother said, "I have a headache. I can't talk now. Why not talk to Second Dharma Brother?"

But the Second Dharma Brother said, "I have a stomach ache, why don't you just go and talk to our Dharma Master?"

So he went back to his master and complained, "Nobody told me anything. Nobody gave me any answers."

But the master said to him reprovingly, "You really are a stupid fool. Everybody has been giving you the answer." Because of this, the disciple reached enlightenment.

WORSE THAN A CLOWN

There was a young monk who was a very serious practitioner of the Dharma.

Once, this monk came across something he did not understand, so he went to ask the master. When the master heard the question, he started laughing loudly. The master then stood up and walked away, still laughing.

The young monk was very disturbed by the master's reaction. For the next three days, he could not eat, sleep nor think properly. At the end of three days, he went back to the master and told the master how disturbed he had felt.

When the master heard this, he said, "Monk, do you know what your problem is? Your problem is that you are worse than a clown!"

The monk was shocked to hear that, "Venerable Sir, how can you say such a thing?! How can I be worse than a clown?"

The master explained, "A clown enjoys seeing people laugh at him. You feel disturbed because another person laughed at you. Tell me, are you not worse than a clown?"

When the monk heard this, he began to laugh. He was enlightened.

A LESSON FROM RYOKAN

There was a Japanese Zen Master called Ryokan. One day, Ryokan heard his family complain that his nephew was wasting money on prostitutes. Ryokan went to visit his nephew, whom he had not seen for many years.

His nephew invited him to stay one night. All night long Ryokan sat in meditation. As he was preparing to leave the next morning, he asked his nephew, "I must be getting old, my hand shakes so. Will you help me tie the string of my straw sandal?"

The nephew helped him.

Ryokan replied, "Thank you. A man gets older and feebler day by day. Take good care of yourself."

Then Ryokan left, without mentioning a word about prostitutes or the complaints of the family. But from that day on, his nephew truly reformed, and stopped spending money on prostitutes and stopped dissipating his life.

SAMSARA AND NIRVANA

"Grief can be the garden of compassion. If you keep your heart open through everything, your pain can become your greatest ally in your life's search for love and wisdom."

—Rumi

A Zen master urged his students to practice diligently in order to transcend the world of birth and death.

A student asked him, "Sir, please tell us how to transcend the world of birth and death."

He said, "You have to look for the world of no birth and no death."

The student asked, "But where can we find the world of no birth and no death?"

"You look for it right in the world of birth and death."

"The Buddha Dharma is in the world,
Awakening is not apart from the world.
If you seek enlightenment apart from the world,
It is like seeking rabbit horns."

—Hui Neng

DELUSION

A man was forcing his way through a thick forest beset with thorns and stones. Suddenly to his great consternation, an elephant appeared and gave chase. He took to his heels through fear, and seeing a well, he ran to hide in it. But to his horror he saw a viper at the bottom of the well. However, lacking other means of escape, he jumped into that well, and clung to a thorny creeper that was growing in it. Looking up, he saw two mice—a white one and a black one—gnawing at the creeper. Over his face there was a beehive from which occasional drops of honey trickled.

This man, foolishly unmindful of this precarious position, was greedily tasting the honey. A kind person volunteered to show him a path of escape. But the greedy man begged to be excused till he had enjoyed himself.

The thorny path is Samsara, the ocean of life. Man's life is not a bed of roses. It is beset with difficulties and obstacles to overcome, with opposition and unjust criticism, with attacks and insults to be borne. Such is the thorny path of life.

The elephant here resembles death; the viper, old age; the creeper, birth; the two mice, night and day. The drop of honey correspond to the fleeting sensual pleasures. The kind person represents the Buddha.

The temporary material happiness is merely the gratification of some desire. When the desired thing is gained, another desire arises. Insatiate are all desires.

'Sorrow is essential to life, and cannot be evaded. Nirvana, being non-conditioned, is [quiescent].'

THE FISH AND THE TURTLE
(Is Nibbana Nothingness?)

Once upon a time there was a fish. And just because it was a fish, it had lived all its life in the water and knew nothing whatever about anything else but water. And one day as it swam about in the lake where all its days had been spent, it happened to meet a turtle of its acquaintance who had just come back from a little excursion on the land.

"Good day, Mr. Turtle!" said the fish. "I have not seen you for a long time. Where have you been?"

"Oh", said the turtle, "I have just been for a trip on dry land."

"On dry land!" exclaimed the fish. "What do you mean by on dry land? There is no dry land. I had never seen such a thing. Dry land is nothing."

"Well," said the turtle good-naturedly. "If you want to think so, of course you may; there is no one who can hinder you. But that's where I've been, all the same."

"Oh, come," said the fish. "Try to talk sense. Just tell me now what is this land of yours like? Is it all wet?"

"No, it is not wet," said the turtle.

"Is it nice and fresh and cool?" asked the fish.

"No, it is not nice and fresh and cool," the turtle replied.

"Is it clear so that light can come through it?"

"No, it is not clear. Light cannot come through it."

"Is it soft and yielding, so that I can move my fins about in it and push my nose through it?"

"No, it is not soft and yielding. You could not swim in it."

"Does it move or flow in streams?"

"No, it neither moves nor flows in streams."

"Does it ever rise up into waves then, with white foams in them?" asked the fish.

"No!" replied the turtle, truthfully. "It never rises up into waves that I have seen."

"There now," exclaimed the fish triumphantly. "Didn't I tell you that this land of yours was just nothing? I have just asked, and you have answered me that it is neither wet nor cool, not clear nor soft and that it does not flow in streams nor rise up into waves. And if it isn't a single one of these things what else is it but nothing? Don't tell me."

"Well, well", said the turtle, "If you are determined to think that dry land is nothing, I suppose you must just go on thinking so. But any one who knows what is water and what is land would say you were just a silly fish, for you think that anything you have never known is nothing just because you have never known it."

And with that the turtle turned away and, leaving the fish behind in its little pond of water, set out on another excursion over the dry land that was nothing.

THE BRAVE LITTLE PARROT

Once, long ago, the Buddha was born as a little parrot. One day a storm fell upon his forest home. Lightning flashed, thunder crashed, and a dead tree, struck by lightning, burst into flames. Sparks leapt on the wind and soon the forest was ablaze. Terrified animals ran wildly in every direction, seeking safety from the flames and smoke.

"Fire! Fire!" cried the little parrot. "To the river!" Flapping his wings, he flung himself out into the fury of the storm and, rising higher, flew towards the safety of the river. But as he flew he could see that many animals were trapped, surrounded by the flames below, with no chance of escape.

Suddenly a desperate idea, a way to save them, came to him.

He darted to the river, dipped himself in the water, and flew back over the now raging fire.

The heat rising up from the burning forest was like the heat of an oven. The thick smoke made breathing almost unbearable. A wall of flames shot up on one side, and then the other. Crackling flames leapt before him. Twisting and turning through the mad maze of fire, the little parrot flew bravely on. At last, when he was over the centre of the forest, he shook his wings and released the few drops of water which still clung to his feathers. The tiny drops tumbled down like jewels into the heart of the blaze and vanished with a hiss.

Then the little parrot once more flew back through the flames and smoke to the river, dipped himself in the cool water, and flew back again over the burning forest. Back and forth he flew, time and time again, from the river to the forest, from the burning forest to the river. His feathers were charred. His feet were scorched. His lungs ached. His eyes, stung by smoke, turned red as coals. His mind spun dizzily as the spinning sparks. But still the little parrot flew on.

At this time, some of the devas — gods of a happy realm — were floating overhead in their cloud palaces of ivory and gold. They happened to look down. And they saw the little parrot flying among the flames. They pointed at him with perfect hands. Between mouthfuls of honeyed foods they exclaimed, "Look at that foolish bird! He's trying to put out a raging forest fire with a few sprinkles of water! How absurd!" And they laughed.

But one of those gods, strangely moved, changed himself into a golden eagle and flew down, down towards the little parrot's fiery path.

The little parrot was just nearing the flames again when the great eagle with eyes like molten gold appeared at his side. "Go back, little bird!" said the eagle in a solemn and majestic voice. "Your task is hopeless! A few drops of water can't put out a forest fire! Cease now and save yourself — before it is too late."

But the little parrot only continued to fly on through the smoke and flames. He could hear the great eagle flying above him as the heat grew fiercer, calling out, "Stop, foolish little parrot! Save yourself! Save yourself!"

"I don't need a great, shining eagle," coughed the little parrot, "to give me advice like that. My own mother, the dear bird, might have told me such things long ago. Advice! (cough, cough), I don't need advice. I just (cough), need someone to help."

And the god, who was that great eagle, seeing the little parrot flying through the flames, thought suddenly of his own privileged kind. He could see them high up above. There they were, the carefree gods, laughing and talking, while many animals cried out in pain and fear from the flames below. And he grew ashamed. Then one single desire was kindled in his heart. God though he was, he just wanted to be like that brave little parrot, and to help.

"I will help!" he exclaimed and, flushed with these new feelings, he began to weep. Stream after stream of sparkling tears poured from his eyes. Wave upon wave, they washed down like cooling rain upon the fire, upon the forest, upon the animals and upon the little parrot himself.

The flames died down and the smoke began to clear. The little parrot, washed and bright, rocketed about the sky laughing for joy. "Now that's more like it!" he exclaimed.

The eagle's tears dripped from burned branches. Smoke rose up from the scorched earth. Miraculously, where those tears glistened, new life pushed forth — fresh shoots, stems, and leaves. Green grass pushed up from among the still glowing cinders.

Where the teardrops sparkled on the parrot's wings, new feathers now grew. Red feathers, green feathers, yellow feathers — such bright colours! Such a handsome bird!

All the animals looked at one another in amazement. They were whole and well. Not one had been harmed. Up above in the clear blue sky they could see their brave friend, the little parrot, looping and soaring in delight. When all hope was gone, somehow he had saved them. "Hurray!" they cried. "Hurray for the brave little parrot and for the miraculous rain!"

THE TAMARIND TREE

One bright and cool summer day the Buddha took a walk along the forest path, simply enjoying the beauty of the earth. At a cross road, he saw a man in grief praying earnestly.

The man recognised the Buddha and fell on his knees. He cried, "Lord Buddha, life is indeed bitter and painful! I was once a man with great wealth, living a life of ease and happiness. By trickery and deceit, those I trusted and loved took everything from me. I am now a wretched man with none to turn to. How many more times must I be reborn into this world of suffering before I can be liberated?"

Pointing to the mango tree by the road, the Buddha said, "Do you see that mango tree? You must be reborn as many times as the number of mangoes on that tree before you know the bliss of liberation from the sufferings of this fleeting world."

Seeing that there are at least dozens of mangoes hanging on the tree, the man gasped, "But Lord! I have lived a righteous life in accord with the precepts! Why am I condemned to suffer so much longer?"

The Buddha sighed. "That is the way it must be." And he continued his walk.

He came across another man praying by the road and this man too, fell on his knees and cried, "Lord Buddha, life is indeed bitter and painful. I have lost all those I loved to the king of death. I am now forlorn and lonely. Life is full of anguish. How many more times must I be reborn into this world of suffering before I know the bliss of liberation?"

The Buddha pointed to the field of wild flowers along the road and said, "Before you know the bliss of liberation from the sufferings of this fleeting world, you must be reborn as many times as the number of flowers in that field."

Seeing so many hundreds of flowers in the field, the man cried, "But Lord! I have done many good deeds and have followed your teachings by heart. Why must I endure so much more suffering?"

The Buddha sighed, "That is how it must be." And he continued on his way.

When he came across a tamarind tree, another man fell down on his knees and cried before him, "Oh Lord! Life is full of suffering! During the days I toiled like a slave under the scathing sun; at night I have nothing to sleep on except a pile of grass on the cold, damped earth. Life is nothing but hunger, thirst and loneliness! How many more times must I be reborn into this world of suffering before I know the bliss of liberation?"

The Buddha looked up to the tamarind tree—each branch of it bearing many stems and each stem has dozens of leaves. The Buddha said, "Look at that tamarind tree. Before you know the bliss of liberation from the sufferings of this fleeting world, you must be reborn as many times as the number of leaves on that tamarind tree."

As the man looked up at the tamarind tree and its thousands of leaves, his eyes filled with tears of gratitude and joy. "How merciful!" he said as he prostrated to the ground at the Buddha's feet.

To this day the tamarind's seeds are the symbol of faithfulness and forbearance.

MIRACULOUS POWER

In Buddhism, it is recognised that supernatural or miraculous power is possible and can be attained through training. However, Buddha Sakyamuni discouraged all display of miraculous power as the proof of spiritual attainment. The following story illustrates the Buddha's attitude towards miraculous powers.

One day the Buddha was waiting by the river bank for a boat to ferry him across the river. An ascetic passed by and proudly showed off his miraculous power, crossing the river back and forth by treading over the water.

The Buddha smiled and asked him, "How long did you train to attain such power?"

"It took me thirty years!", said the ascetic.

The Buddha replied, "Thirty years? Well, I can cross the river using the boat for only one penny!"

If a wicked man can become a pure religious man, this according to Buddhism, is a practical miracle.

GODDESS OF WEALTH
AND GODDESS OF POVERTY

Once a beautiful and well-dressed woman visited a house. The master of the house asked her who she was; and she replied that she was the goddess of wealth. The master of the house was delighted and so greeted her with open arms. Soon after another woman appeared who was ugly looking and poorly dressed. The master asked who she was and the woman replied that she was the goddess of poverty.

The master was frightened and tried to drive her out of the house, but the woman refused to depart, saying, 'The goddess of wealth is my sister. There is an agreement between us that we are never to live apart; if you chase me out, she is to go with me.' Sure enough, as soon as the ugly woman went out, the other woman disappeared.

Birth goes with death. Fortune goes with misfortune. Bad things follow good things. Everyone should realise this. Foolish people dread misfortune and strive after good fortune, but those who seek Enlightenment must transcend both of them and be free of worldly attachment.

YAJNADATTA THE MAD MAN

The Shurangama Sutra relates the story of Yajnadatta, the mad man of Shravasti, who one day looked in the mirror and noticed that the person reflected in it had a head. At that point, he lost his reason and said, 'How come that person has a head and I don't? Where has my head gone?' He then ran wildly through the streets asking everyone he met, 'Have you seen my head? Where has it gone?' He accosted everyone he met, yet no one knew what he was doing. 'He already has a head,' they said. 'What's he looking for another one for?'

There are a lot of people just like poor Yajnadatta.
— Master Hsuan Hua

THE HUMAN CONDITION/STOP THE TRAIN

A man, being late for a trip, arrived at a railroad station and jumped onto the first available train. He dozed off for a while and then upon waking up, saw the train rumbling along at full speed toward an unknown destination. He began querying everyone, complaining aloud and finally crying and shouting. He demanded that the train stop to let him off. The more excited he became, the more the other passengers, eerily silent and sowncast, seemed puzzled by his behaviour. Finally a kind old man told him, "don't you know, this train has only one destination, the ocean depths from which no one ever returns." Once we are born, our final destination is death — the deep ocean. Why fret and fuss? All we can do is to use our time on earth to develop the Bodhi-mind, seeking Enlightenment for ourselves and others.

THE POWER OF KEEPING THE PRECEPTS

Formerly, in Kubhana state (Kashmir), there was nearby a monastery a poisonous dragon which frequently played havoc in the region.

In the monastery five hundred arhats gathered together but failed to drive away the dragon with their collective power of Dhyana-samadhi. Later, a monk came to the monastery where he did not enter into Dhyana-samadhi; he merely said to the poisonous dragon: 'Will the wise and virtuous one leave this place and go to some distant one.' Thereupon, the poisonous dragon fled to a distant place.

When asked by the arhats what miraculous power he had used to drive away the dragon, the monk replied: 'I did not use the power of Dhyana-samadhi; I am only very careful about keeping the rules of discipline and I observe a minor one with the same care as a major one.'

So, we can see that the collective power of five hundred arhats' Dhyana—samadhi cannot compare with a monk's strict observance of the rules of discipline.

THE STORY OF THE HOE

A farmer plowed the land with a hoe day after day, year after year. The work was hard, but the harvest was plentiful. And yet, one day he couldn't help but ask himself, "Why am I working so hard? Life is meaningless and boring! Where is my life heading?"

Shortly afterwards, a monk came to his house to ask for alms. The monk looked free and happy, which deeply impressed the farmer. Being a monk and living an unencumbered life seemed admirable. Yes, what a good idea! The farmer cheerfully made up his mind to give up everything and become a monk.

As soon as he left his house, he suddenly felt how empty his hands were. He was so used to holding a hoe in his hands to work that without the hoe he now felt a little lost. Therefore, he went back to his house, picked up his hoe, and tried hard to think of what he could do with it. It was a fine hoe. The shaft was smooth and shiny from daily use. It would be heartbreaking to throw it away.

"OK, then," he thought, "I'll wrap it up and put it away." He found a secure place in the house to hide it. Now everything was settled. With his mind at ease, the farmer left his house at last.

The farmer did all he could to fulfill the requirements to be a true monk. However, he could hardly resist thinking of his hoe whenever he came across green paddies. Every now and then, he would rush back home just to feel the hoe and then return to the temple.

Time passed by quickly. After seven or eight years, he felt that something was missing. "Why haven't I fulfilled my dream of becoming a free, happy monk after having tried

45

very hard to cultivate my morality? There is something I haven't let go of. Now it's time to get rid of my burden!" He rushed back home, picked up the hoe and threw it into a lake. Splash, there it went! "I won! I succeeded!" he couldn't resist crying out loud.

Just at that moment, a king, leading his victorious army, happened to pass by. He overheard the cry and went to ask the monk, "What did you win? Why are you so cheerful?" "I have conquered the devils in my heart. I have let all my burdens go."

The king saw that the monk was really happy and free from earthly burdens and delusions. The king thought to himself, "Now I've won the war. Victory is mine. But am I really happy? I took lands that didn't belong to me. It is not real victory." Then and there, the king realised that although he had won the war, he was not a real winner, but a common person burdened with life's vexations. He realised that in order to become a real winner and a saint, you have to conquer the devils in your heart.

TRUTH

"Sometime, somewhere you take something to be the truth. If you cling to it so much, when the truth comes in person and knocks at your door, you will not open it." — Buddha.

There was a young widower who loved his seven-year-old son very much. One day he went away to a distant city on business. While he was gone, a band of bandits came and burned down his whole village. They took away his son, together with the properties looted. When the young man returned and saw the ruins, he was devastated. Running and screaming, he took the charred corpse of a child to be his own son. He lost his reason and began to pull his hair and pound on his chest, crying uncontrollably. After the cremation, he collected the ashes, put them in a beautiful bag and carried it with him all the time, no matter where he went or what he did. One night when he was crying on the bed holding the bag of ashes, someone knocked on his door rapidly. It was his true son who has escaped from the bandits and found his way home. Barely raising his voice, he asked, "Who's that?" And the child answered, "It's me, papa! Open the door, it's me!" In his confused and agitated state of mind, the man thought that someone must be playing mischief with him. He shouted for the child to go away, clutching the bag to his chest as tightly as he could and continue to cry. His true son knocked on the door again and again, but the father simply refused to even go out and check. Finally, the child left.

From that time on, father and son never saw each other again.

THREE QUESTIONS

IT once occurred to a certain king, that if he always knew the right time to begin everything; if he knew who were the right people to listen to, and whom to avoid, and, above all, if he always knew what was the most important thing to do, he would never fail in anything he might undertake.

And this thought having occurred to him, he had it proclaimed throughout his kingdom that he would give a great reward to any one who would teach him what was the right time for every action, and who were the most necessary people, and how he might know what was the most important thing to do.

And learned men came to the King, but they all answered his questions differently.

In reply to the first question, some said that to know the right time for every action, one must draw up in advance, a table of days, months and years, and must live strictly according to it. Only thus, said they, could everything be done at its proper time. Others declared that it was impossible to decide beforehand the right time for every action; but that, not letting oneself be absorbed in idle pastimes, one should always attend to all that was going on, and then do what was most needful. Others, again, said that however attentive the King might be to what was going on, it was impossible for one man to decide correctly the right time for every action, but that he should have a Council of wise men, who would help him to fix the proper time for everything.

But then again others said there were some things which could not wait to be laid before a Council, but about which one had at once to decide whether to undertake them or not. But in order to decide that one must know beforehand what was going to happen. It is only magicians who know that; and, therefore in order to know the right time for every action, one must consult magicians.

Equally various were the answers to the second question. Some said, the people the King most needed were his councillors; others, the priests; others, the doctors; while some said the warriors were the most necessary.

To the third question, as to what was the most important occupation: some replied that the most important thing in the world was science. Others said it was skill in warfare; and others, again, that it was religious worship.

All the answers being different, the King agreed with none of them, and gave the reward to none. But still wishing to find the right answers to his questions, he decided to consult a hermit, widely renowned for his wisdom.

The hermit lived in a wood which he never quitted and he received none but common folk. So the King put on simple clothes, and before reaching the hermit's cell dismounted from his horse, and, leaving his bodyguard behind, went on alone.

When the King approached, the hermit was digging the ground in front of his hut. Seeing the King, he greeted him and went on digging. The hermit was frail and weak, and each time he stuck his spade into the ground and turned a little earth, he breathed heavily.

The King went up to him and said: 'I have come to you, wise hermit, to ask you to answer three questions: How can I learn to do the right thing at the right time? Who are the people I most need, and to whom should I, therefore, pay more attention than to the rest? And, what affairs are the most important and need my first attention?'

The hermit listened to the King, but answered nothing. He just spat on his hand and recommenced digging.

'You are tired,' said the King, 'let me take the spade and work awhile for you.'

'Thanks!' said the hermit, and, giving the spade to the King, he sat down on the ground.

When he had dug two beds, the King stopped and repeated his questions. The hermit again gave no answer, but rose, stretched out his hand for the spade, and said:

'Now rest awhile — and let me work a bit.'

But the King did not give him the spade, and continued to dig. One hour passed, and another. The sun began to sink behind the trees, and the King at last stuck the spade into the ground, and said:

'I came to you, wise man, for an answer to my questions. If you can give me none, tell me so, and I will return home.'

'Here comes some one running,' said the hermit, 'let us see who it is.'

The King turned round, and saw a bearded man come running out of the wood. The man held his hands pressed against his stomach, and blood was flowing from under them. When he reached the King, he fell fainting on the ground moaning feebly. The King and the hermit unfastened the man's clothing. There was a large wound in his stomach. The King washed it as best he could, and bandaged it with his handkerchief and with a towel the hermit had. But the blood would not stop flowing, and the King again and again removed the bandage soaked with warm blood, and washed and rebandaged the wound. When at last the blood ceased flowing, the man revived and asked for something to drink. The King brought fresh water and gave it to him. Meanwhile the sun had set, and it had become cool. So the King, with the hermit's help, carried the wounded man into the hut and laid him on the bed. Lying on the bed the man closed his eyes and was quiet; but the King was so tired with his walk and with the work he had done, that he crouched down on the threshold, and also fell asleep — so soundly that he slept all through the short summer night. When he awoke in the morning, it was long before he could remember where he was, or who was the strange bearded man lying on the bed and gazing intently at him with shining eyes.

'Forgive me!' said the bearded man in a weak voice, when he saw that the King was awake and was looking at him.

'I do not know you, and have nothing to forgive you for,' said the King.

'You do not know me, but I know you. I am that enemy of yours who swore to revenge himself on you, because you executed his brother and seized his property. I knew you had gone alone to see the hermit, and I resolved to kill you on your way back. But the day passed and you did not return. So I came out from my ambush to find you, and I came upon your bodyguard, and they recognised me, and wounded me. I escaped from them, but should have bled to death had you not dressed my wound. I wished to kill you, and you have saved my life. Now, if I live, and if you wish it, I will serve you as your most faithful slave, and will bid my sons do the same. Forgive me!'

The King was very glad to have made peace with his enemy so easily, and to have gained him for a friend, and he not only forgave him, but said he would send his servants and his own physician to attend him, and promised to restore his property.

Having taken leave of the wounded man, the King went out into the porch and looked around for the hermit. Before going away he wished once more to beg an answer to the questions he had put. The hermit was outside, on his knees, sowing seeds in the beds that had been dug the day before.

The King approached him, and said:

'For the last time, I pray you to answer my questions, wise man.'

'You have already been answered!' said the hermit still crouching on his thin legs, and looking up at the King, who stood before him.

'How answered? What do you mean?' asked the King.

'Do you not see,' replied the hermit. 'If you had not pitied my weakness yesterday, and had not dug these beds for me, but had gone your way, that man would have attacked you, and you would have repented of not having stayed with me. So the most important time was when you were digging the beds; and I was the most important man; and to do me good was your most important business. Afterwards, when that man ran to us, the most important time was when you were attending to him, for if you had not bound up his wounds he would have died without having made peace with you. So he was the most important man, and what you did for him was your most important business. Remember then: there is only one time that is important — Now! It is the most important time because it is the only time when we have any power. The most necessary man is he with whom you are, for no man knows whether he will ever have dealings with any one else: and the most important affair is, to do him good, because for that purpose alone was man sent into this life!'

BECAUSE I'M HERE

An old monk was sweeping the yard in a monastery under the scorching sun.

Another monk passed by and asked him, "How old are you?"

The old monk replied, "I'm seventy-seven."

"You are so old! Why are you still working so hard here?"

"Well, because I'm here."

"But why are you working under the scorching sun?"

"Because the sun is there."

Act without worrying about the results, and strive for excellence without dwelling on it. If we put all of our hearts into what we do without complaining, we can become one with the "Way."

THE MONKEY KING

There was once a kingdom of monkeys in the forest. The King of the Monkeys was very very large, and was very kind and wise. One day, the King was strolling and he noticed mango trees along the side of a river. He also noticed a human castle downstream. He then ordered the monkeys to remove all the mangos from these trees, "or there would be disaster". The monkeys did not understand the King's intention, but they did as told anyway. All the mangos were taken off these trees except one. This one was hidden behind a nest.

One day, this mango was ripe and fell into the river. It flowed downstream where the human King was having a bath. He noticed the mango and asked the Prime Minister what it was. The Prime Minister told him it was a 'mango', a fruit of wonderful taste. The King then ordered that the mango be cut into small pieces and he gave a small piece to each of his ministers. When satisfied that the mango was not poisonous, he ate the rest of it and realised how tasty it was. He craved for more.

The next day, the human king, with his troops, went upstream to search for more of these fruits. There were lots of mango trees, but also lots of monkeys. The human king doesn't want to share the mangos with the monkeys, so he ordered all of them to be killed. A massacre started.

When the news reached the wise Monkey King, he commented, "The day has finally arrived". The thousands of monkeys were chased all the way to the edge of the forest. There was a deep cliff at the edge of the forest, and a bamboo forest at the other side of the cliff. The Monkey King saw that if his subjects could cross over to the bamboo forest, they will be saved.

With his huge body, he formed a bridge over the cliff and thousands of monkeys trampled over him to reach the safety of the bamboo forest. He endured all the pain. One monkey did not like the King and he saw this as an opportunity to get even. As he was crossing over the King's body, he pierced a spear through the King's heart. The King screamed in pain but endured the pain until all his subjects were safely across. Then he collapsed.

The human king witnessed the whole thing. He was so touched that he ordered the Monkey King be saved. When the Monkey King recovered his consciousness, the human king asked him, "You are their King, why did you bother to die for them?". The Monkey King replied, "Because I am their King". With that, he died.

The human king was so touched that he decided to be a good king from that day and he ordered that the monkeys in the bamboo forest be protected from harm forever.

CARRYING AND LEAVING

Once upon a time, there were two monks who went on a pilgrimage across the country together. One day, they came to a river bank and saw a beautiful girl who was unable to cross the river.

Seeing her difficulty, the elder monk volunteered to carry her across the river on his back while the younger one looked on in consternation.

When the sun went down, the monks came upon a dilapidated shack and decided to stay there for the night. The elder monk quickly fell asleep while the younger one twisted around, unable to calm his mind. Finally, he woke up the elder monk and reprimanded him for what happened during the day, "As monks, we are supposed to keep away from women. I am really ashamed and troubled by what you did today!"

The elder monk looked at his friend and a smile broke up on his face, "Oh, so that has been bothering you! Brother, I have left the girl behind by the river bank, why are you still carrying her around?"

ESARHADDON, KING OF ASSYRIA

The Assyrian King, Esarhaddon, had conquered the kingdom of King Lailie, had destroyed and burnt the towns, taken all the inhabitants captive to his own country, slaughtered the warriors, beheaded some chieftains and impaled or flayed others, and had confined King Lailie himself in a cage.

As he lay on his bed one night, King Esarhaddon was thinking how he should execute Lailie, when suddenly he heard a rustling near his bed, and opening his eyes saw an old man with a long grey beard and mild eyes.

"You wish to execute Lailie?" asked the old man.

"Yes," answered the King. "But I cannot make up my mind how to do it."

"But you are Lailie," said the old man.

"That's not true," replied the King. "Lailie is Lailie, and I am I."

"You and Lailie are one," said the old man. "You only imagine you are not Lailie, and that Lailie is not you."

"What do you mean by that?" said the King. "Here am I, lying on a soft bed; around me are obedient men-slaves and women-slaves, and tomorrow I shall feast with my friends as I did today; whereas Lailie is sitting like a bird in a cage, and tomorrow he will be impaled, and with his tongue hanging out will struggle till he dies, and his body will be torn in pieces by dogs."

"You cannot destroy his life," said the old man.

"And how about the fourteen thousand warriors I killed, with whose bodies I built a mound?" said the King. "I am alive, but they no longer exist. Does not that prove that I can destroy life?"

"How do you know they no longer exist?"

"Because I no longer see them. And, above all, they were tormented, but I was not. It was ill for them, but well for me."

"That, also, only seems so to you. You tortured yourself, but not them."

"I do not understand," said the King.

"Do you wish to understand?"

"Yes, I do."

"Then come here," said the old man, pointing to a large font full of water.

The King rose and approached the font.

"Strip, and enter the font."

Esarhaddon did as the old man bade him.

"As soon as I begin to pour this water over you," said the old man, filling a pitcher with the water, "dip down your head."

The old man tilted the pitcher over the King's head and the King bent his head till it was under water.

And as soon as King Esarhaddon was under the water he felt that he was no longer Esarhaddon, but some one else. And, feeling himself to be that other man, he saw himself lying on a rich bed, beside a beautiful woman. He had never seen her before, but he knew she was his wife. The woman raised herself and said to him:

"Dear husband, Lailie! You were wearied by yesterday's work and have slept longer than usual, and I have guarded your rest, and have not roused you. But now the Princes await you in the Great Hall. Dress and go out to them."

And Esarhaddon — understanding from these words that he was Lailie, and not feeling at all surprised at this, but only wondering that he did not know it before — rose, dressed, and went into the Great Hall where the Princes awaited him.

The Princes greeted Lailie, their King, bowing to the ground, and then they rose, and at his word sat down before him; and the eldest of the Princes began to speak, saying that it was impossible longer to endure the insults of the wicked King Esarhaddon, and that they must make war on him. But Lailie disagreed, and gave orders that envoys shall be sent to remonstrate with King Esarhaddon; and he dismissed the Princes from the audience. Afterwards he appointed men of note to act as ambassadors, and impressed on them what they were to say to King Esarhaddon. Having finished this business, Esarhaddon — feeling himself to be Lailie — rode out to hunt wild asses. The hunt was successful. He killed two wild asses himself, and having returned home, feasted with his friends, and witnessed a dance of slave girls. The next day he went to the Court, where he was awaited by petitioners suitors, and prisoners brought for trial; and there as usual he decided the cases submitted to him. Having finished this business, he again rode out to his favourite amusement: the hunt. And again he was successful: this time killing with his own hand an old lioness, and capturing her two cubs. After the hunt he again feasted with his friends, and was entertained with music and dances, and the night he spent with the wife whom he loved.

So, dividing his time between kingly duties and pleasures, he lived for days and weeks, awaiting the return of the ambassadors he had sent to that King Esarhaddon who used to be himself. Not till a month had passed did the ambassadors return, and they returned with their noses and ears cut off.

King Esarhaddon had ordered them to tell Lailie that what had been done to them — the ambassadors — would be done to King Lailie himself also, unless he sent immediately a tribute of silver, gold, and cypress-wood, and came himself to pay homage to King Esarhaddon.

Lailie, formerly Esarhaddon, again assembled the Princes, and took counsel with them as to what he should do. They all with one accord said that war must be made against Esarhaddon, without waiting for him to attack them. The King agreed; and taking his place at the head of the army, started on the campaign. The campaign lasts seven days. Each day the King rode round the army to rouse the courage of his warriors. On the eighth day his army met that of Esarhaddon in a broad valley through which a river flowed. Lailie's army fought bravely, but Lailie, formerly Esarhaddon, saw the enemy swarming down from the mountains like ants, over-running the valley and overwhelming his army; and, in his chariot, he flung himself into the midst of the battle, hewing and felling the enemy. But the warriors of Lailie were but as hundreds, while those of Esarhaddon were as thousands; and Lailie felt himself wounded and taken prisoner. Nine days he journeyed with other captives, bound, and guarded by the warriors of Esarhaddon. On the tenth day he reached Nineveh, and was placed in a cage. Lailie suffered not so much from hunger and from his wound as from shame and impotent rage. He felt how powerless he was to avenge himself on his enemy for all he was suffering. All he could do was to deprive his enemies of the pleasure of seeing his sufferings; and he firmly resolved to endure courageously without a murmur, all they could do to him. For twenty days he sat in his cage, awaiting execution. He saw his relatives and friends led out to death; he heard the groans of those who were executed:

some had their hands and feet cut off, others were flayed alive, but he showed neither disquietude, nor pity, nor fear. He saw the wife he loved, bound, and led by two black eunuchs. He knew she was being taken as a slave to Esarhaddon. That, too, he bore without a murmur. But one of the guards placed to watch him said, "I pity you, Lailie; you were a king, but what are you now?" And hearing these words, Lailie remembered all he had lost. He clutched the bars of his cage, and, wishing to kill himself, beat his head against them. But he had not the strength to do so and, groaning in despair, he fell upon the floor of his cage.

At last two executioners opened his cage door, and having strapped his arms tight behind him, led him to the place of execution, which was soaked with blood. Lailie saw a sharp stake dripping with blood, from which the corpse of one of his friends had just been torn, and he understood that this had been done that the stake might serve for his own execution. They stripped Lailie of his clothes. He was startled at the leanness of his once strong, handsome body. The two executioners seized that body by its lean thighs; they lifted him up and were about to let him fall upon the stake.

"This is death, destruction!" thought Lailie, and, forgetful of his resolve to remain bravely calm to the end, he sobbed and prayed for mercy. But no one listened to him.

"But this cannot be," thought he. "Surely I am asleep. It is a dream." And he made an effort to rouse himself, and did indeed awake, to find himself neither Esarhaddon nor Lailie — but some kind of an animal. He was astonished that he was an animal, and astonished, also, at not having known this before.

He was grazing in a valley, tearing the tender grass with his teeth, and brushing away flies with his long tail. Around him was frolicking a long-legged, dark-gray ass-colt, striped down its back. Kicking up its hind legs, the colt galloped full speed to Esarhaddon, and poking him under the stomach with its smooth little muzzle, searched for the teat, and, finding it, quieted down, swallowing regularly. Esarhaddon understood that he was a she-ass, the colt's mother, and this neither surprised nor grieved him, but rather gave him pleasure. He experienced a glad feeling of simultaneous life in himself and in his offspring.

But suddenly something flew near with a whistling sound and hit him in the side, and with its sharp point entered his skin and flesh. Feeling a burning pain, Esarhaddon —who was at the same time the ass — tore the udder from the colt's teeth, and laying back his ears galloped to the herd from which he had strayed. The colt kept up with him, galloping by his side. They had already nearly reached the herd, which had started off, when another arrow in full flight struck the colt's neck. It pierced the skin and quivered in its flesh. The colt sobbed piteously and fell upon its knees. Esarhaddon could not abandon it, and remained standing over it. The colt rose, tottered on its long, thin legs, and again fell. A fearful two-legged being — a man — ran up and cut its throat.

"This cannot be; it is still a dream! thought Esarhaddon, and made a last effort to awake. "Surely I am not Lailie, nor the ass, but Esarhaddon!"

He cried out, and at the same instant lifted his head out of the font. The old man was standing by him, pouring over his head the last drops from the pitcher.

"Oh, how terribly I have suffered! And for how long!" said Esarhaddon.

"Long?" replied the old man, "you have only dipped your head under water and lifted it again; see, the water is not yet all out of the pitcher. Do you now understand?"

Esarhaddon did not reply, but only looked at the old man with terror.

"Do you now understand," continued the old man, "that Lailie is you, and the warriors you put to death were you also? And not the warriors only, but the animals which you slew when hunting and ate at your feasts were also you. You thought life dwelt in you alone but I have drawn aside the veil of delusion, and have let you see that by doing evil to others you have done it to yourself also. Life is one in them all, and yours is but a portion of this same common life. And only in that one part of life that is yours, can you make life better or worse — increasing or decreasing it. You can only improve life in yourself by destroying the barriers that divide your life from that of others, and by considering others as yourself, and loving them. By so doing you increase your share of life. You injure your life when you think of it as the only life, and try to add to its welfare at the expense of other lives. By so doing you only lessen it. To destroy the life that dwells in others is beyond your power. The life of those you have slain has vanished from your eyes, but is not destroyed. You thought to lengthen your own life and to shorten theirs, but you cannot do this. Life knows neither time nor space. The life of a moment, and the life of a thousand years: your life and the life of all the visible and invisible beings in the world, are equal. To destroy life, or to alter it, is impossible; for life is the one thing that exists. All else, but seems to us to be."

Having said this the old man vanished.

Next morning King Esarhaddon gave orders that Lailie and

all the prisoners should be set at liberty and that the executions should cease.

On the third day he called his son Assur-bani-pal, and gave the kingdom over into his hands; and he himself went into the desert to think over all he had learnt. Afterwards he went about as a wanderer through the towns and villages, preaching to the people that all life is one, and that when men wish to harm others, they really do evil to themselves.

PRAJNA

A monk once asked: "Is Prajna great?"

The Master answered: "Yes, it is."

The monk asked: "How great?"

The Master answered: "Boundless."

The monk asked: "Is Prajna small?"

The Master answered: "Yes, it is."

The monk asked: "How small?"

The Master answered: "So small you can't see it."

The monk asked: "Then where is it?"

The Master answered: "Where is it not?"

YOU ARE ALSO CORRECT

Two monks who came out of a lecture by their master went on a hot debate regarding what they heard during the lecture. Each of them insisted that his understanding was the correct one. To settle the dispute, they went to see the master for a judgement.

After hearing the argument put forth by the first monk, the master said, "You are correct!" The monk was overjoyed. Casting a winner's glance at his friend, he left the room.

The second monk was upset and started to pour out what he thought to the master. After he finished, the master looked at him and said, "You are correct, too." Hearing this, the second monk brightened up and went away.

A third monk who was also in the room was greatly puzzled by what he saw. He said to the master, "I am confused, master! Their positions regarding the issue are completely opposite. They can't be both right! How could you say that they are both correct?"

The master smiled as he looked into the eyes of this third monk, "You are also correct!"

THE USELESS EYEBROWS

Once, a person's eyes, nose, and mouth had a meeting. First the eyes said, "We, the eyes, are of utmost importance to the body. Everything must be seen by us to know whether it is beautiful or not, big or small, tall or short. Without eyes, walking around will be very difficult. So we, the eyes, are very important. But we have been improperly placed under the eyebrows, which are of no use. It is just not fair!"

Next, the nose said, "I, the nose, am the most important. Only I can distinguish a good smell from a foul odour. The act of breathing is also dependent on me. If I do not let the breath pass through, everybody will die. So I am the most important. As important as I am, I have been unfairly placed beneath the useless eyebrows. I am most unhappy."

Then the mouth said, "I am the most important part of the human body. I can speak; if not for me, there would not be any communication among people. I take in the food; if not for me, everybody would die of hunger. Such an important part as myself has been placed in the lowest part of the face. The useless eyebrows, however, have been put on the highest part of the face. This I cannot accept!"

After the others had spoken, the eyebrows spoke slowly, "Please do not fight anymore. We, the eyebrows, are surely the most useless things; we admit defeat. We are willing to be placed below you." Having said this, the eyebrows settled down below the eyes. Unfortunately, the person no longer looked like a human being. Next, they eyebrows settled down below the nose. It was still horrible; it still did not look like a human being. Then the eyebrows settled down below the mouth. This looked even more ghastly! The eyes, nose, and mouth huddled to discuss the situation again. They concluded that it was best if the eyebrows returned to their original place on the face; it was the most appropriate spot for them. When the eyebrows returned to their original spot, the appearance was once again that of a human being. Thus, we can see that what appears to be the most useless thing can be indeed the most useful.

THE WAY

A person asking Ch'an Master Wei K'uan, "Where is the Way?"

"Right before your eyes."

"Why do I not see it?"

"You do not see it because you have the notion of a self."

"Because I have the notion of a self, I do not see it. Has the Master seen it?"

"The notion of 'you,' in addition to the notion of a self, further keeps you from seeing."

"If there is neither the notion of 'you' nor the notion of a self, can it be seen?"

"If there is neither 'you' nor 'a self,' then who wants to see it?"

MAN WOUNDED BY ARROW

A man had been wounded by an arrow thickly smeared with poison, and his friends and kinsmen went to get a surgeon to heal him, and he said, I will not have this arrow pulled out until I know by what man I was wounded, whether he is of the warrior caste, or a brahmin, or of the agricultural, or the lowest caste. If he were to say, I will not have this arrow pulled out until I know of what name of family the man is — or whether he is tall, or short or of middle height. Before knowing all this, the man would die.

Similarly, it is not on the view that the world is eternal, that it is finite, that body and soul are distinct, or that the Buddha exists after death that a religious life depends. Whether these views or their opposite are held, there is still rebirth, there is old age, there is death, and grief, lamentation, suffering, sorrow, and despair. I have not spoken to these views because they do not conduce to an absence of passion, to tranquillity, and Nirvana. And what have I explained? Suffering have I explained, the cause of suffering, the destruction of suffering, and the path that leads to the destruction of suffering have I explained. For this is useful.

THE STORY OF UPALI

On one occasion Upali the millionaire, a follower of Nigantha Nataputta, approached the Buddha and was so pleased with the Buddha's exposition of the Dhamma that he instantly expressed his desire to become a follower of the Buddha. But the Buddha advised him, saying— "Of a verity, O householder, make a thorough investigation. It is well for a distinguished man like you to make a thorough investigation."

Upali, who was overwhelmed with joy at this unexpected utterance of the Buddha. said: "Lord, if I had become a follower of another teacher, his followers would have taken me round the streets in procession proclaiming that such and such a millionaire had renounced his former religion and had embraced theirs. But, Lord, you advise me to investigate further. The more pleased am I with this salutary advise of yours." And he appreciatively repeated— for the second time, "I seek refuge in the Buddha, the Dhamma, and the Sangha."

Though Upali became a Buddhist by conviction, the Buddha, quite in keeping with his boundless compassion and perfect tolerance, advised him to support his former religious teacher in accordance with his practice.

A CHAN MASTER'S TEAR

One day, Ch'an Master K'ung-yeh was travelling on the road and met some bandits who wanted to rob him.

Tears fell from the Master's eyes.

The bandits started laughing and exclaimed, "What a coward!"

Master K'ung-yeh then said, "Don't think that I'm crying because I'm afraid of you. I am not even afraid of birth and death. I feel sorry for you young people. You are strong and healthy, yet instead of doing things that are beneficial for others, you hurt people by robbing them. Of course, what you are doing is not acceptable and cannot be tolerated by society. What is worse is that you will all go to hell and suffer great pain. I am so worried about you that I cannot restrain myself and am shedding tears for you"

The bandits were moved and decided to give up their evil ways.

KISA GOTAMI

Kisa Gotami was the wife of a wealthy man of Savatthi. She had only one child. When her son was old enough to start running about, he caught a disease and died. Kisa Gotami was greatly saddened. Unable to accept that her son was dead and could not be brought back to life again, she took him in her arms and went about asking for medicine to cure him. Everyone she encountered thought that she had lost her mind. Finally, an old man told her that if there was anyone who could help her, it would be the Buddha.

In her distress, Kisa Gotami brought the body of her son to the Buddha and asked him for a medicine that would bring back his life. The Buddha answered: "I shall cure him if you can bring me some white mustard seeds from a house where no one has died".

Carrying her dead son, she went from door to door, asking at each house. At each house the reply was always that someone had died there. At last the truth struck her, "No house is free from death". She laid the body of her child in the wood and returned to the Buddha,

who comforted her and preached to her the truth. She was awakened and entered the first stage of Arhatship. Eventually, she became an Arhat.

RAINY DAY, SUNNY DAY

There was once an old lady who cried all the time. Her elder daughter was married to an umbrella merchant while the younger daughter was the wife of a noodle vendor. On sunny days, she worried, "Oh no! The weather is so nice and sunny. No one is going to buy any umbrellas. What will happen if the shop has to be closed?" These worries made her sad. She just could not help but cry. When it rained, she would cry for the younger daughter. She thought, "Oh no! My younger daughter is married to a noodle vendor. You cannot dry noodles without the sun. Now there will be no noodles to sell. What should we do?" As a result, the old lady lived in sorrow everyday. Whether sunny or rainy, she grieved for one of her daughters. Her neighbours could not console her and jokingly called her "the crying lady."

One day, she met a monk. He was very curious as to why she was always crying. She explained the problem to him. The monk smiled kindly and said, "Madam! You need not worry. I will show you a way to happiness, and you will need to grieve no more."

The crying lady was very excited. She immediately asked the monk to show her what to do. The master replied, "It is very simple. You just need to change your perspective. On sunny days, do not think of your elder daughter not being able to sell umbrellas but the younger daughter being able to dry her noodles. With such good strong sunlight, she must be able to make plenty of noodles and her business must be very good. When it rains, think about the umbrella store of the elder daughter. With the rain, everyone must be buying umbrellas. She will sell a lot of umbrellas and her store will prosper."

The old lady saw the light. She followed the monks instruction. After a while, she did not cry anymore; instead, she was smiling everyday. From that day on she was known as "the smiling lady."

WHAT DID BODHIDHARMA BRING WHEN HE CAME FROM THE WEST?

There was a monk who asked his master, "What did Bodhidharma bring when he came from the West?"

The master replied, "He didn't bring anything."

The monk insisted, "Didn't Bodhidharma bring Buddhadharma, the teaching of Buddha, from the West?"

The master replied, "No, not really. Buddhadharma has always been in China."

The monk was puzzled, "Well, that's strange then. If Buddhadharma was already here, why did Bodhidharma bother coming to China?"

The master replied, "Because Buddhadharma was already here, it is for that reason that Bodhidharma had to leave India and come here."

DEER AND TIGER

The mountains were splendid. But Wu Tang didn't care a whit for scenery. He and his son spent a lot of time hunting in these mountains. Wu Tang was a dead shot with his bow and arrow. He never missed. He was such a good shot that he barely had to aim. He just picked a target, pulled his bow, and shot it down. No animal was quick enough or agile enough to escape his arrows. Look, over there, a little fawn! A little fawn must be one of the most adorable animals in nature, but Wu Tang wasn't in the mountains to admire nature. As soon as he spotted it, he whipped an arrow out of his quiver and zoom! The fawn fell over dead. Then Wu noticed its mother a few feet away in the grass. He couldn't get a good shot at her from his angle, so he waited. She was terribly sad about her little baby! She let out a cry as she started licking her baby's wounds. Just as she was concentrating on that, Wu pulled off a quick shot and the mother deer died on the spot.

But that wasn't enough for Wu. He thought there might be more deer in the area, because he heard something rustling around in the grass. There was at least one more in there, maybe two. "Three deer is better than two," he thought, as he prepared. Then he located the source of the sound and shot at a shadow in the grass. He was proud to hear the sound of another dead body falling to the ground, but his pride turned to anguish when he heard a groan! Deer don't groan like that! That was a human voice! Wu rushed over and saw that his third shot had killed not a deer, but his own son, who had come out hunting with him!

Wu was stupefied. He seemed to hear a voice telling him, "Wu Tang! Now do you now what it is like to see your baby shot to death with an arrow? Animals love their young as much as you do. How much anguish have you caused animal parents!" Wu stood there, numb, too heartbroken to pay attention to a sound that came from the side. Then in a flash he realised that the other animal he had heard in the grass was not a deer, but a tiger! But he was too late.

BEGINNER'S MIND

Once, a professor went to a Zen Master. He asked him to explain the meaning of Zen. The Master quietly poured a cup of tea. The cup was full but he continued to pour.

The professor could not stand this any longer, so he questioned the Master impatiently, "Why do you keep pouring when the cup is full?"

"I want to point out to you," the Master said, "that you are similarly attempting to understand Zen while your mind is full. First, empty your mind of preconceptions before you attempt to understand Zen."

"If your mind is empty, it is always ready for anything; it is open to everything. In the beginner's mind there are many possibilities, in the expert's mind there are few."

—Suzuki Roshi

THE YOUNG MONK WHO SAVED THE ANTS

Once upon a time in the deep mountains forest there lived an old monk and a young monk. The old monk was a great practitioner of Buddha-dharma and was frequently in deep meditation. Normally when he started meditation, it could last for half a day or one full day. In addition, during his meditation he would know what was going to happen in the future.

One day, the old monk meditated again. Suddenly he found out that his little disciple was going to pass away in eight days. Therefore the old monk called the young monk and said,

"My child, I am going to give you an eight-day holiday so that you can go home to see your mother and father."

"Really? That's very good, thank you Shifu."

In fact, lately I have been feeling quite homesick too."

"However, you must remember to come back here by the eighth day."

"Okay, Shifu, please take care of yourself. I am leaving now."

"Go home now!"

Delightedly the young monk went down the mountains, without realising that in the eyes of the old monk, there was sadness and a sense of reluctance to see him leave. After a long walk, the young monk stopped at the bank of the stream to drink some water as he was getting thirsty. Then he saw there was an ant cave in which countless ants were going into and out of it. He stayed to observe for a while with interest. When he was just about to leave,

"Oh! Why is the water level of the stream rising? Oh no!! The ants will be drowned!!"

The reason was it had been raining upstream for a few days continuously. Therefore the water level downstream was starting to rise.

He quickly took off his cloth and he put some hard soil in it to made up a protection wall along the cave. Not only did he managed to stop water from covering the cave, but also skilfully diverted the flow of the water to somewhere else.

Hence he saved the lives of countless ants. Eight days passed quickly. The old monk was strolling in the mountains forest sadly. Suddenly from a distance, he saw the little monk coming back up to the mountains cheerfully. Happily he asked the young monk to recount what he had done in the past eight days while he had been away. When he pondered on this story he finally understood that because the young monk had saved the lives of countless ants this had caused his fated eight-day life expectancy to lengthen into a long and happy life.This is the merit of cultivating good deeds, however seemingly insignificant they be.

THE SOUND THE HARE HEARD

One morning while some bhikkhus were on their alms round in Savatthi, they passed some ascetics of different sects practicing austerities. Some of them were naked and lying on thorns. Others sat around a blazing fire under the burning sun.

Later, while the monks were discussing the ascetics, they asked the Buddha, "Lord, is there any virtue in those harsh ascetic practices?"

The Buddha answered, "No, monks, there is neither virtue nor any special merit in them. When they are examined and tested, they are like a path over a dunghill, or like the noise the hare heard."

Puzzled, the monks said, "Lord, we do not know about that noise. Please tell us what it was."

At their request the Buddha told them this story of the distant past.

Long, long ago, when Brahmadatta was reigning in Baranasi, the Bodhisatta was born as a lion in a forest near the Western Ocean. In one part of that forest there was a grove of palms mixed with belli trees. A hare lived in that grove beneath a palm sapling at the foot of a belli tree.

One day the hare lay under the young palm tree, idly thinking, "If this earth were destroyed, what would become of me?" At that very instant a ripe belli fruit happened to fall and hit a palm leaf making a loud "THUD!"

Startled by this sound, the hare leapt to his feet and cried, "The earth is collapsing!" He immediately fled, without even glancing back.

Another hare, seeing him race past as if for his very life, asked, "What's wrong?" and started running, too.

"Don't ask!" panted the first. This frightened the second hare even more, and he sprinted to keep up.

"What's wrong?" he shouted again.

Pausing for just a moment, the first hare cried, "The earth is breaking up!" At this, the two of them bolted off together.

Their fear was infectious, and other hares joined them until all the hares in that forest were fleeing together. When other animals saw the commotion and asked what was wrong, they were breathlessly told, "The earth is breaking up!" and they too began running for their lives. In this way, the hares were soon joined by herds of deer, boars, elk, buffaloes, wild oxen, and rhinoceroses, a family of tigers, and some elephants.

When the lion saw this headlong stampede of animals and heard the cause of their flight, he thought, "The earth is certainly not coming to an end. There must have been some sound which they misunderstood. If I don't act quickly they will be killed. I must save them!"

Then, as fast as only he could run, he got in front of them, and roared three times. At the sound of his mighty voice, all the animals stopped in their tracks. Panting, they huddled together in fear. The lion approached and asked why they were running away.

"The earth is collapsing," they all answered.

"Who saw it collapsing?" he asked.

"The elephants know all about it," some animals replied.

When he asked the elephants, they said, "We don't know. The tigers know."

The tigers said, "The rhinoceroses know."

The rhinoceroses said, "The wild oxen know."

The wild oxen said, "The buffaloes know."

The buffaloes said, "The elk know."

The elk said, "The boars know."

The boars said, "The deer know."

The deer said, "We don't know. The hares know."

When he asked the hares, they pointed to one particular hare and said, "This one told us."

The lion asked him, "Is it true, sir, that the earth is breaking up?"

"Yes, sir, I saw it," said the hare.

"Where were you when you saw it?"

"In the forest in a palm grove mixed with belli trees. I was lying there under a palm at the foot of a belli tree, thinking, 'If this earth were destroyed, what would become of me?' At that very moment I heard the sound of the earth breaking up and I fled."

From this explanation, the lion realised exactly what had really happened, but he wanted to verify his conclusions and demonstrate the truth to the other animals. He gently calmed the animals and said, "I will take the hare and go to find out whether or not the earth is coming to an end where he says it is. Until we return, stay here."

Placing the hare on his tawny back, he raced with great speed back to that grove. Then he put the hare down and said,

"Come, show me the place you meant."

"I don't dare, my lord," said the hare.

"Don't be afraid," said the lion.

The hare, shivering in fear, would not risk going near

the belli tree. He could only point and say, "Over there, sir, is the place of dreadful sound."

The lion went to the place the hare indicated. He could make out where the hare had been lying in the grass, and he saw the ripe belli fruit that had fallen on the palm leaf. Having carefully ascertained that the earth was not breaking up, he placed the hare on his back again and returned to the waiting animals.

He told them what he had found and said, "Don't be afraid." Reassured, all the animals returned to their usual places and resumed their routines.

Those animals had placed themselves in great danger because they listened to rumours and unfounded fears rather than trying to find out the truth themselves. Truly, if it had not been for the lion, those beasts would have rushed into the sea and perished. It was only because of the Bodhisatta's wisdom and compassion that they escaped death.

At the conclusion of the story, the Buddha identified the Birth: "At that time, I myself was the lion."

So that a disheartened bhikkhu would have no regrets in the future, the Buddha told him this story at Savatthi to encourage him to persevere. "If you give up your practice in this sublime teaching which leads to Nibbana," the Buddha told him, "you will suffer long, like the trader of Seriva who lost a golden bowl worth a hundred thousand pieces."

When asked to explain, the Buddha told this story of the distant past.

Five long aeons ago, the Bodhisatta was an honest trader selling fancy goods in the kingdom of Seriva. Sometimes he travelled with another trader from the same kingdom, a greedy fellow, who handled the same wares.

One day the two of them crossed the Telavaha river to do business in the bustling city of Andhapura. As usual, to avoid competing with each other, they divided the city between them and began selling their goods from door to door.

In that city there was a ramshackle mansion. Years before the family had been rich merchants, but by the time of this story their fortunes had dwindled to nothing, and all the men of the family had died. The sole survivors were a girl and her grandmother, and these two earned their living by working for hire.

That afternoon, while the greedy peddler was on his rounds, he came to the door of that very house, crying, "Beads for sale! Beads for sale!"

When the young girl heard his cry, she begged, "Please buy me a trinket, Grandmother."

"We're very poor, dear. There's not a cent in the house and I can't think of anything to offer in exchange."

The girl suddenly remembered an old bowl. "Look!" she cried. "Here's an old bowl. It's of no use to us. Let's try to trade it for something nice."

What the little girl showed her grandmother was an old bowl which had been used by the great merchant, the late head of the family. He had always eaten his curries served from this beautiful, expensive bowl. After his death it had been thrown among the pots and pans and forgotten. Since it hadn't been used for a very long time, it was completely covered with grime. The two women had no idea it was gold.

The old woman asked the trader to come in and sit down. She showed him the bowl and said, "Sir, my granddaughter would like a trinket. Would you be so kind as to take this bowl and give her something or other in exchange?"

The peddler took the bowl in his hand and turned it over. Suspecting its value, he scratched the back of it with a needle. After just one covert look, he knew for certain the bowl was real gold.

He sat there frowning and thinking until his greed got the better of him. At last he decided to try to get the bowl without giving the woman anything whatever for it. Pretending to be angry, he growled, "Why did you bring me this stupid bowl? It isn't worth half a cent!" He threw the bowl to the floor, got up, and stalked out of the house in apparent disgust.

Since it had been agreed between the two traders that the one might try the streets which the other had already covered, the honest peddler came later into that same street and appeared at the door of the house, crying, "Beads for sale!"

Once again the young girl made the same request of her grandmother, and the old woman replied, "My dear, the first peddler threw our bowl on the ground and stormed out of the house. What have we got left to offer?"

"Oh, but that trader was nasty, Grandmother. This one looks and sounds very kind. I think he will take it."

"All right, then. Call him in."

When the peddler came into the house, the two women gave him a seat and shyly put the bowl into his hands. Immediately recognising that the bowl was gold, he said, "Mother, this bowl is worth a hundred thousand pieces of silver. I'm sorry but I don't have that much money."

Astonished at his words, the old woman said, "Sir, another peddler who came here a little while ago said that it was not worth half a cent. He got angry, threw it on the floor, and went away. If it wasn't valuable then, it must be because of your own goodness that the bowl has turned into gold. Please take it, and just give us something or other for it. We will be more than satisfied."

At that time the peddler had only five hundred pieces of silver and goods worth another five hundred. He gave everything to the women, asking only to keep his scales, his bag, and eight coins for his return fare. Of course, they were happy to agree. After profuse thanks on both sides, the trader hurried to the river with the golden bowl. He gave his eight coins to the boatman and got into the boat.

Not long after he had left, the greedy peddler returned to the house, giving the impression of having reluctantly reconsidered their offer. He asked them to bring out their bowl, saying he would give them something or other for it after all.

The old woman flew at him. "You scoundrel!" she cried.

"You told us that our golden bowl was not worth even half a cent. Lucky for us, an honest trader came after you left and told us it was really worth a hundred thousand pieces of silver. He gave us a thousand for it and took it away, so you are too late!"

When the peddler heard this, an intense pain swept over him. "He robbed me! He robbed me!" he cried. "He got my golden bowl worth a hundred thousand!" He became hysterical and lost all control. Throwing down his money and merchandise, he tore off his shirt, grabbed the beam of his scales for a club, and ran to the riverside to catch the other trader.

By the time he got to the river, the boat was already in midstream. He shouted for the boat to return to shore, but the honest peddler, who had already paid, calmly told the ferryman to continue on.

The frustrated trader could only stand there on the river-bank and watch his rival escape with the bowl. The sight so infuriated him that a fierce hate swelled up inside him. His heart grew hot, and blood gushed from his mouth. Finally, his heart cracked like the mud at the bottom of a pond dried up by the sun. So intense was the unreasoning hatred which he developed against the other trader because of the golden bowl, that he perished then and there.

The honest trader returned to Seriva, where he lived a full life spent in charity and other good works, and passed away to fare according to his deserts.

When the Buddha finished this story, he identified himself as the honest trader, and Devadatta as the greedy trader. This was the beginning of the implacable grudge which Devadatta held against the Bodhisatta through innumerable lives.

THE MASSACRE OF THE SAKYA CLANSMEN

Before the advent of Sakyamuni Buddha, there was near Kapila town a village inhabited by fishermen, and in it was a big pond. It happened that because of a great drought, the pond ran dry and all the fish were caught and eaten by the villagers. The last fish taken was a big one and before it was killed, a boy who never ate fish, played with it and thrice knocked its head.

Later, after Sakyamuni Buddha's appearance in this world, King Prasenajit who believed in the Buddha-dharma, married a Sakya girl who then gave birth to a prince called Crsytal. When he was young, Crystal had his schooling in Kapila which was then inhabited by the Sakya clansmen. One day while playing, the boy ascended to the Buddha's seat and was reprimanded by others who dragged him down. The boy cherished a grudge against the men and when he became king, he led his soldiers to attack Kapila, killing all its inhabitants.

At the same time, the Buddha suffered from a headache which lasted three days. When His disciples asked Him to rescue the poor inhabitants, the Buddha replied that a fixed Karma could not be changed. By means of his miraculous powers, Maudgalyayana rescued five hundred Sakya clansmen and thought he could give them refuge in his own bowl which was raised up in the air. When the bowl was brought down, all the men had been turned into blood.

When asked by His chief disciples, the Buddha related the story of the villagers who in days gone by had killed all the fish in their pond; King Crystal had been the big fish and his soldiers the other fish in the pond; the inhabitants of Kapila who were now killed had been those who ate the fish; and the Buddha Himself had been the boy who thrice knocked the head of the big fish. Karma was now causing Him to suffer from a headache for three days in retribution for his previous act. Since there could be no escape from the effects of a fixed Karma, the five hundred Sakya clansmen, although rescued by Maudgalyayana, shared the same fate. Later, King Crystal was reborn in a hell.

As cause produces effect which in turn becomes a new cause the retribution is inexhaustible. The law of causality is really very dreadful.

MILAREPA'S LAST TESTAMENT

After the enlightened cave-yogi and songmaster Milarepa left this world, a scrap of rice paper was found inscribed with his handwriting. His ascetic followers were astounded, for it stated that beneath a nearby boulder was buried all the gold that ascetic Mila had hoarded during his life.

A few eager disciples dug around and under that large rock. In the earth they discovered a ragged cloth bundle. Opening the knotted bundle with shaking hands, they discovered only a lump of dried shit.

There was another scribbled note as well. It said: "If you understand my teaching so little that you actually believed I ever valued or hoarded gold, you are truly heirs to my shit."

The note was signed "The Laughing Vajra, Milarepa."

KUNALA

After Buddha passed away, there was a king named Usika. He was very kind and his government was very compassionate. He had a son with eyes as beautiful as the kunala, an Indian bird famous for its beautiful eyes. Because the king liked this kind of bird, he named his son Kunala. When Prince Kunala grew up, he was very handsome. His conduct was proper and he was very kind.

King Usika was a devoted Buddhist. One day, the king brought his son to a temple, and he asked a monk named Yasa about the Buddhist teachings. Yasa looked at the young prince. "Human life is impermanent," he said. "A body goes through the stages of birth, aging, illness and death, and human life is filled with impurity. Who can have the beauty of youth forever? All these are illusions. In the same way, although the prince's eyes seem beautiful, they are actually full of filth and the source of trouble."

The prince was quite puzzled. Everyone always praised him for his beautiful eyes, but why would the monk say that they were dirty and the source of trouble? These words kept whirling around in his head.

There were many concubines in the king's palace. One young lady was deeply attracted by Kunala's good looks. When she saw him sitting alone in the garden one day, she started to fondle him, trying to seduce him. But the prince was a righteous person and could not agree to such behaviour. He pulled himself together and freed himself from her unwanted attentions.

Later, when the young prince was old enough to marry, King Usika found a wife for him. When the concubine saw the lover of her dreams married to someone else, she became intensely jealous and her love turned to hatred.

Not long after the marriage, the king became sick and the young concubine looked after him carefully until he recovered. He was grateful for her care and said to her, "Because you took care of me for such a long time, I will give you anything you desire."

She said, "I just want to rule the country for seven days." The king thought to himself that since he had promised, he couldn't go back on his word. Besides, it was only for seven days. So he agreed.

When she was on the throne, the young lady wrote a letter filled with both love and hate and sent it to Prince Kunala. She wrote that her fury would only be placated if she never saw his eyes again. Now the prince finally realised what that monk had meant, but it was too late. The lady's word was like the king's command, and it couldn't be disobeyed.

Kunala reluctantly gouged out one eye and held it in his hand. "It's so disgusting," he suddenly realised. "Why would such a filthy little thing be praised by so many people and bring so much trouble? Since she wants both eyes, I'll take out the other one too." When both eyes were gone, everything before him was in total darkness, but his mind was suddenly filled with light. He felt the peace that comes from spiritual exaltation.

When his wife heard the news, she ran to the blind prince and started to wail with grief. But the prince was calm and consoled her with the Buddhist teachings. "Human life is impermanent, so don't harbour hatred or worry, because hatred and worry are your greatest enemies."

At that time, a bodyguard warned the prince, "Your Highness, if you stay in the palace, I'm afraid that your life will be in danger." The prince, of course, was already aware of this, and since he didn't want the court lady to continue making bad karma for herself by doing something even worse, he and his wife fled the palace. They learned to play the lute and to sing, and they wandered from town to town, making music in the streets. People would throw them a few coins, and in this way, the prince and his wife were able to feed themselves.

A few years later, they happened to come back to the capital. One day, they wandered into the streets alongside the palace and started to sing. When King Usika heard the beautiful but mournful songs, he thought of his son, who had suddenly disappeared years before. He told his attendant to invite the musicians to enter the palace.

When the king saw the lute player, he realised that it was indeed the son that he had been thinking of day and night. When he saw how Prince Kunala had fallen from his royal life and was now only a blind lute-player singing on the streets for a living, the king was very distressed. He asked the prince, "Who did this to you? Who made you lose your sight?" But Kunala refused to talk about it. He just told his father about the truths that he had learned, hoping his father would calm down.

At last, the ministers and the guards couldn't endure it any more and reported the truth to the king. He was furious and wanted to execute that concubine, but the prince begged his father to forgive her.

The king was touched by Prince Kunala's compassion and released the young concubine. However, in her own conscience, she was ashamed of herself and finally committed suicide. Because of her impure love, she had created trouble and hatred, hurt other people and destroyed herself. Was it all worth it?

EIGHT EARTHLY WINDS

There was a well-known scholar who practiced Buddhism and befriended a Chan master. Thinking that he had made great stride in his cultivation, he wrote a poem and asked his attendant to deliver it to the Chan master who lived across the river. The master opened the letter and read the short poem aloud:

"Unmoved by the Eight Worldly Winds,[1]
Serenely I sit on the purplish gold terrace."

A smile broke up on the lips of the master. Picking up an ink brush, he scribbled the word "farting" across the letter and asked that it be delivered back to the scholar.

The scholar was upset and went across the river right away to reprimand the master for being rude. The master laughed as he said, "You said you are no longer moved by the Eight Worldly Winds and yet with just one word of 'farting', you ran across the river like a rat!"

[1] Eight Worldly Winds/Conditions: Gain and loss, fame and defame, praise and blame, happiness and pain.

THE GOING FOURTH

I will describe the Going Forth,
how he, the One-with-Vision, went forth,
how he reasoned and chose the Going Forth.
"Household life is crowded,
a realm of dust,
while going forth
is the open air."
Seeing this, he went forth.

On going forth,
he avoided evil deeds in body.
Abandoning verbal misconduct,
he purified his livelihood.
Then he, the Buddha, went to Rajagaha,
the mountain fortress of the Magadhans,
and wandered for alms,
endowed with all the foremost marks.
King Bimbisara, standing in his palace,
saw him, and on seeing him, consummate in marks,
said: "Look at this one, sirs.
How handsome, stately, pure!
How consummate his demeanour!
Mindful, his eyes downcast,
looking only a plow-length before him,
as one who's not from a lowly lineage:
Send the royal messengers at once
to see where this monk will go."

They — the messengers dispatched —
followed behind him.
"Where will this monk go?
Where will his dwelling place be?"
As he went from house to house —

well-restrained, his sense-doors guarded,
mindful, alert — his bowl filled quickly.
Then he, the sage, completing his alms round,
left the city, headed for Mount Pandava.
"That's where his dwelling will be."
Seeing him go to his dwelling place,
three messengers sat down,
while one returned to tell the king.
"That monk, your majesty,
on the flank of Pandava,
sits like a tiger, a bull,
a lion in a mountain cleft."

Hearing the messenger's words,
the noble warrior king
straight away went by royal
coach, out to Mount Pandava.
Going as far as the coach would go,
he got down, went up on foot,
and on arrival sat down.
Sitting there,
he exchanged courteous greetings,
then said:
"You are young, youthful,
in the first stage of youth,
endowed with the stature & colouring
of a noble-warrior.
You would look glorious
in the vanguard of an army,
arrayed with an elephant squadron.
I offer you wealth: enjoy it.
I ask your birth: inform me."

"Straight ahead, your majesty,
by the foothills of the Himalayas,

is a country consummate
in energy & wealth,
inhabited by Kosalans:
Solar by clan,
Sakyans by birth.
From that lineage I have gone forth,
but not in search of sensual pleasures.
Seeing the danger in sensual pleasures
— and renunciation as rest —
I go to strive.
That's where my heart delights."

I have heard that on one occasion the Blessed One was staying in Savatthi at Jeta's Grove, Anathapindika"s park. There he addressed the monks,

"Monks!"

"Yes, lord," the monks replied.

The Blessed One said: "Monks, speech endowed with four characteristics is well-spoken, not poorly spoken — faultless and not to be faulted by the wise. Which four? There is the case where a monk says only what is well-spoken, not what is poorly spoken; only what is just, not what is unjust; only what is endearing, not what is unendearing; only what is true, not what is false. Speech endowed with these four characteristics is well-spoken, not poorly spoken — faultless & not to be faulted by the wise."

That is what the Blessed One said. Having said this, the One Well-Gone, the Teacher, said further:

The calm say that what is well-spoken is best;
second, that one should say
what is just, not unjust;
third, what's endearing, not unendearing;

fourth, what is true, not false.

Then Ven. Vangisa, rising from his seat, arranging his robe over one shoulder, faced the Blessed One with his hands palm-to-palm in front of his heart and said, "An inspiration has come to me, Blessed One! An inspiration has come to me, One Well-Gone!"

"Let the inspiration come to you, Vangisa," the Blessed One said.

Then Ven. Vangisa praised the Blessed One to his face with these attractive verses:

Speak only the speech
that neither torments self
nor does harm to others.
That speech is truly well spoken.

Speak only endearing speech,
speech that is welcomed.
Speech when it brings no evil
to others
is pleasant.

Truth, indeed, is deathless speech:
This is an ancient principle.
The goal and the Dhamma
— so say the calm —
are firmly established on truth.

The speech the Awakened One speaks,
for attaining Unbinding,
rest,
for making an end
to the mass of stress:
That is the speech unexcelled.

A HEAP OF BONES

This was said by the Lord:

"Bhikkhus, the skeletons of a single person, running on and wandering in samsara for an aeon, would make a heap of bones, a quantity of bones as large as this Mount Vepulla, if there were someone to collect them and if the collection were not destroyed."

> The bones of a single person
> Accumulated in a single aeon
> Would make a heap like a mountain —
> So said the Great Sage.
>
> He declared it to be
> As great as Mount Vepulla
> To the north of Vulture's Peak
> In the hill-fort of Magadha.
>
> But when one sees with perfect wisdom
> The four noble truths as they are —
> Suffering, the origin of suffering,
> The overcoming of suffering,
> And the noble eightfold path
> Leading to relief from suffering —
>
> Having merely run on
> Seven times at the most,
> By destroying all fetters
> One makes an end of suffering.

GIVING

This was said by the Lord:

"Bhikkhus, if beings knew, as I know, the result of giving and sharing, they would not eat without having given, nor would they allow the stain of meanness to obsess them and take root in their minds. Even if it were their last morsel, their last mouthful, they would not eat without having shared it, if there were someone to share it with. But, bhikkhus, as beings do not know, as I know, the result of giving and sharing, they eat without having given, and the stain of meanness obsesses them and takes root in their minds."

> If beings only knew —
> So said the Great Sage —
> How the result of sharing
> Is of such great fruit,
> With a gladdened mind,
> Rid of the stain of meanness,
> They would duly give to noble ones
> Who make what is given fruitful.
>
> Having given much food as offerings
> To those most worthy of offerings,
> The donors go to heaven
> On departing the human state.
> Having gone to heaven they rejoice,
> And enjoying pleasures there,
> The unselfish experience the result
> Of generously sharing with others.

THE DEVELOPMENT OF LOVING KINDNESS

This was said by the Lord:

"Bhikkhus, whatever grounds there are for making merit productive of a future birth, all these do not equal a sixteenth part of the mind-release of loving-kindness. The mind-release of loving-kindness surpasses them and shines forth, bright and brilliant.

"Just as the radiance of all the stars does not equal a sixteenth part of the moon's radiance, but the moon's radiance surpasses them and shines forth, bright and brilliant, even so, whatever grounds there are for making merit productive of a future birth, all these do not equal a sixteenth part of the mind-release of loving-kindness.

"Just as in the last month of the rainy season, in the autumn, when the sky is clear and free of clouds, the sun, on ascending, dispels the darkness of space and shines forth, bright and brilliant, even so, whatever grounds there are for making merit productive of a future birth, all these do not equal a sixteenth part of the mind-release of loving-kindness.

"And just as in the night, at the moment of dawn, the morning star shines forth, bright and brilliant, even so, whatever grounds there are for making merit productive of a future birth, all these do not equal a sixteenth part of the mind-release of loving-kindness. The mind-release of loving-kindness surpasses them and shines forth, bright and brilliant."

For one who mindfully develops
Boundless loving-kindness
Seeing the destruction of clinging,
The fetters are worn away.

If with an uncorrupted mind
He pervades just one being
With loving kindly thoughts,
He makes some merit thereby.

But a noble one produces
An abundance of merit
By having a compassionate mind
Towards all living beings.

Those royal seers who conquered
The earth crowded with beings
Went about performing sacrifices:
The horse sacrifice, the man sacrifice,
The water rites, the soma sacrifice,
And that called "the Unobstructed."

But these do not share even a sixteenth part
Of a well cultivated mind of love,
Just as the entire starry host
Is dimmed by the moon's radiance.

One who does not kill
Nor cause others to kill,
Who does not conquer
Nor cause others to conquer,
Kindly towards all beings —
He has enmity for none.

This too is the meaning of what was said by the Lord,
so I heard.

THE NOT-BORN

This was said by the Lord:

"There is, bhikkhus, a not-born, a not-brought-to-being, a not-made, a not-conditioned. If, bhikkhus, there were no not-born, not-brought-to-being, not-made, not-conditioned, no escape would be discerned from what is born, brought-to-being, made, conditioned. But since there is a not-born, a not-brought-to-being, a not-made, a not-conditioned, therefore an escape is discerned from what is born, brought-to-being, made, conditioned."

The born, come-to-be, produced,
The made, the conditioned, the transient,
Conjoined with decay and death,
A nest of disease, perishable,
Sprung from nutriment and craving's cord —
That is not fit to take delight in.

The escape from that, the peaceful,
Beyond reasoning, everlasting,
The not-born, the unproduced,
The sorrowless state that is void of stain,
The cessation of states linked to suffering,
The stilling of the conditioned — bliss.

THE NIBBANA-ELEMENT

This was said by the Lord.

"Bhikkhus, there are these two Nibbana-elements. What are the two? The Nibbana-element with residue left and the Nibbana-element with no residue left.

"What, bhikkhus, is the Nibbana-element with residue left? Here a bhikkhu is an arahant, one whose taints are destroyed, the holy life fulfilled, who has done what had to be done, laid down the burden, attained the goal, destroyed the fetters of being, completely released through final knowledge. However, his five sense faculties remain unimpaired, by which he still experiences what is agreeable and disagreeable and feels pleasure and pain. It is the extinction of attachment, hate, and delusion in him that is called the Nibbana-element with residue left.

"Now what, bhikkhus, is the Nibbana-element with no residue left? Here a bhikkhu is an arahant... completely released through final knowledge. For him, here in this very life, all that is experienced, not being delighted in, will be extinguished. That, bhikkhus, is called the Nibbana-element with no residue left.

"These, bhikkhus, are the two Nibbana-elements."

These two Nibbana-elements were made known
By the Seeing One, stable and unattached:
One is the element seen here and now
With residue, but with the cord of being destroyed;
The other, having no residue for the future,
Is that wherein all modes of being utterly cease.
Having understood the unconditioned state,

Released in mind with the cord of being destroyed,

They have attained to the Dhamma-essence.

Delighting in the destruction (of craving),

Those stable ones have abandoned all being.

CASTLES IN THE SAND

Some children were playing beside a river. They made castles of sand, and each child defended his castle and said, 'This one is mine.' They kept their castles separate and would not allow any mistakes about which was whose. When the castles were all finished, one child kicked over someone else's castle and completely destroyed it. The owner of the castle flew into a rage, pulled the other child's hair, struck him with his fist and bawled out, 'He has spoiled my castle! Come along all of you and help me punish him as he deserves.' The others all came to his help. They beat the child. Then they went on playing in their sand castles, each saying, 'This is mine; no one else may have it. Keep away! Don't touch my castle!'

But evening came, it was getting dark and they all thought they ought to be going home. No one now cared what became of his castle. One child stamped on his, another pushed his over with both hands. Then they turned away and went back, each to his home.

HELD BY VIEWS

This was said by the Lord:

"Bhikkhus, held by two kinds of views, some devas and human beings hold back and some overreach; only those with vision see.

"And how, bhikkhus, do some hold back? Devas and humans enjoy being, delight in being, are satisfied with being. When Dhamma is taught to them for the cessation of being, their minds do not enter into it or acquire confidence in it or settle upon it or become resolved upon it. Thus, bhikkhus, do some hold back.

"How, bhikkhus, do some overreach? Now some are troubled, ashamed, and disgusted by this very same being and they rejoice in (the idea of) non-being, asserting: 'In as much as this self, good sirs, when the body perishes at death, is annihilated and destroyed and does not exist after death — this is peaceful, this is excellent, this is reality!' Thus, bhikkhus, do some overreach.

"How, bhikkhus, do those with vision see? Herein a bhikkhu sees what has come to be as having come to be. Having seen it thus, he practices the course for turning away, for dispassion, for the cessation of what has come to be. Thus, bhikkhus, do those with vision see."

> Having seen what has come to be
> As having come to be,
> Passing beyond what has come to be,
> They are released in accordance with truth
> By exhausting the craving for being.
>
> When a bhikkhu has fully understood
> That which has come to be as such,

Free from craving to be this or that,
By the extinction of what has come to be
He comes no more to renewal of being.

This too is the meaning of what was said by the Lord, so I heard.

RECOVERING A SMALL DEBT

A merchant lent another person half a string of cash. But a long time went by, and his debtor had still not paid back the loan. So he went to collect his debt. On the way, he had to cross a river, and no ferry across, he had to pay two strings of cash. However, when he got to the debtor's house, the man wasn't in. On the return trip, he had to pay the boatman another two strings of cash.

To spent four strings of cash in order to get back half a string, not to mention the weariness of the long journey, is to spend much for little. No wonder everyone jeered at his foolishness.

THE WIFE WHO PRETENDED SHE HAD DIED

A foolish man cherished a deep love for his beautiful wife, but she was a flippant woman. Soon, she fell in love with another man and was ready to desert her husband for him.

Day day, she secretly told an old woman, "After I'm gone, put the body of a dead woman in my room. Then tell my husband that I've died." Sure enough, after she left, the old woman dragged a dead body into her house while the husband was away. When he returned, she told him that his wife had died in the meantime. The man ran to look at the corpse and thinking it was his wife's, he cried in sorrow and got some firewood and fuel to cremate the body. He put the ashes into a small bag which he kept with him day and night.

Some time later, the wife got tired of her lover and returned home. She told the man she was his wife, but the husband replied, "My wife died a long time ago. Who are you and how dare you utter such nonsense?" No matter how the wife tried to explain, he would not listen.

EATING HALF A PIE WOULD BE QUITE ENOUGH

A man was so hungry that he was ready to eat seven pies. But he felt quite full after he had eaten six and a half. He regretted this so much that he started to beat himself, exclaiming, "I am full because I ate the last half piece of pie. The other six pieces were wasted.

Had I known that half a pie would be enough, I should have eaten it first."

THE GREAT MATTER OF BIRTH AND DEATH

In India there was once a king who believed in a non-Buddhist religion which taught many kinds of bitter practices ...some spread ashes on their bodies, and some slept on beds of nails. They cultivated all kinds of ascetic practices. Meanwhile, the Bhikshus who cultivated the Buddhadharma had it 'easy,' because they didn't cultivate that way. Now, the king of that country said to the Buddha's disciples, 'It's my belief that the ascetic practices which these non-Buddhists cultivate still don't enable them to end their afflictions. How much the less must you Bhikshus, who are so casual, be able to sever the affliction of your thoughts of sexual desire.'

One of the Dharma Masters answered the king this way: 'Suppose you take a man from jail who had been sentenced to execution, and you say to him 'Take this bowl of oil and carry it in your two hands as you walk down the highway. If you don't spill a single drop, I'll release you when you return.' Then, suppose you send some beautiful women musicians out on the highway to sing and play their instruments where the sentenced man is walking with his bowl of oil. If he should spill any oil, of course, you'll execute him. But if he should come back without spilling a single drop, what do you suppose he will answer if you ask him what he's seen on the road?'

The king of country did just that: he took a man destined to be executed and said to him, 'Today you should be executed but I'm going to give you an opportunity to save your life. How? I'll give you a bowl of oil to carry in your two hands as you take a walk on the highway. If you can do it without spilling a single drop, I'll spare your life.

Go try it.' The sentenced man did as he was told. He went out on the highway, and when he returned he had not spilled one drop. Then the king asked him, 'What did you see out on the highway?' The sentenced man said, 'I didn't see a single thing. All I did was watch the oil to keep it from spilling. I didn't see anything else or hear anything at all.'

So, the king asked the Dharma Master, 'Well, what is the principle here?' The Dharma Master answered, 'The sentenced man was like the novice who has left the home life. Both see the question of Birth and Death as too important to waste time on thoughts of sexual desire, the most dangerous affliction for ascetics.

Why can't people sever their afflictions? Because they don't understand Birth and Death. They don't realise how great the importance of this matter is and therefore, are not single-minded in their determination to transcend it.'

FORGIVE AND FORGET

During the Ch'ing Dynasty in China, in Yang Chou, there was a person named Ch'eng Pai Lin. One day he had a dream in which Avalokitesvara Bodhisattva told him, 'Tomorrow the Ch'ing army will arrive. Out of the seventeen people in your household, sixteen will survive. But you cannot escape your fate. Tomorrow Wang Ma Tze will kill you, because in a past life you stabbed him twenty-six times and killed him.' Then Avalokitesvara Bodhisattva added, 'There is still an expedient method that may work. Prepare a fine feast tomorrow, and when he comes, invite him to eat with you. Afterwards, allow him to kill you. Perhaps that will change things.'

The dream was vivid and when Ch'eng Pai Lin awoke the following morning, he went out and bought wine and vegetables, brought them back, and had a feast prepared. Then noontime came, someone knocked at the door. He opened the door and said, 'Are you Wang Ma Tze?' 'How strange,' said the man at the door, 'I'm from the north, how did you know my name?' His host invited him in and said, '... You're welcome; I've prepared a feast for you. Won't you join me?' Then he related the dream he'd had the night before. 'Last life I killed you with twenty-six stabs of a knife, and so this life you have come to kill me. After we've finished this meal, you can do it.' Wang Ma Tze pondered over this and said, 'But if you killed me last life, and I kill you this life, won't you kill me again next life? It will just go on and on. No, I won't kill you.' Then he took his knife and scratched twenty-six marks on his hosts back to represent that the debt had been repaid.

Not only did Wang Ma Tze not kill his host, but afterwards they became very good friends. Wang said to his host, 'The Ch'ing army is following en masse. They are not reasonable, so the best would be for you and your family to go to Su Chou. It's safe there.' So that is what Ch'eng Pai Lin did. This is a case of turning grievance into friendship and reversing the retribution that is due one. From this you can see that it's possible to alter one's fate."

'He beat me, he robbed me. Look at how he abused and injured me.' Live with those thoughts and you will never stop hating... Abandon such thoughts and your hatred and suffering will cease."

CAUSE AND EFFECT
ILLEGITIMATE CHILD

Once, it is said, Buddha Sakyamuni was falsely accused of fathering a certain woman's child. When the deceit was discovered, the Buddha's followers wanted to beat the culprit to death. The Buddha calmly stopped them, saying: "Oh, Bhikkus, in a previous lifetime when I was a king, I was once in a grove together with my courtiers. At the sight of an ascetic, the ladies of the party surrounded him, turning their backs on me. Jealous and angry, I exclaimed, How do you know that this ascetic is not a fake? How do you know that he does not spend his nights revelling with women? It is because of that slanderous remark that I have now had to endure that woman's deceit. Oh, monks, release her and let her go in peace."

In the Buddhist world view, nothing happens without cause. To transcend suffering, we must stop causing further suffering. Acting otherwise is no different than trying to escape one's shadow by running in the blazing sun!

CULTIVATION
MIND EMPTY & STILL

Once upon a time there was a Zen monk who practiced in a deserted mountain area.

Lonely and isolated, he had a deluded thought, wishing to have some fellow monks practicing along with him to make life more bearable. Immediately, an old woman appeared from nowhere, leading two beautiful young girls by the hand, who, she said, lived in the village down in the valley. They had come to seek guidance in the Way. The monk, unsuspicious, immediately gave a Dharma talk to the group. One day, after many such visits over a period of time, the old woman respectfully requested that the two girls be allowed to become attendants to the monk and relieve him of his daily chores. The monk, hearing this, became suspicious. He reprimanded the old woman severely and refused the offer. The three women left, looking angry and ashamed.

The monk, intrigued, followed them discreetly until they disappeared around a bend in the road. When he reached the spot, he found it was a dead end with no habitation or anything else around, except for three very old trees, one big tree and two smaller ones. He thought it over and realised that he had been 'tested.' A fleeting thought occurred to him, that he should cut down the trees, start a bonfire, and burn them to the ground. At that moment, the three women reappeared, repentant, begging him to forgive them and spare their lives.

Therefore, the cultivator should remember: when the mind is still, all realms are calm; when delusion arises, demons are born.

FAULT-FINDING
GOOD SPIRITUAL ADVISOR

According to the Brahma Net and Avatamsaka Sutras, we should ignore appearances and external forms when seeking a good teacher. For example, we should disregard such traits as youth, poverty, low status or lack of education, unattractive appearance or incomplete features, but should simply seek someone conversant with the Dharma, who can be of benefit to us. Nor should we find fault with good spiritual advisors for acting in certain ways, as it may be due to a number of reasons, such as pursuing a hidden cultivation practice or following an expedient teaching. Or else, they may act the way they do because while their achievements may be high, their residual bad habits have not been extinguished. If we grasp at forms and look for faults, we will forfeit benefits on the path of cultivation.

Thus, when Buddha Sakyamuni was still alive, the Bhikshu Kalodayin was in the habit of moving his jaws like a buffalo; a certain Bhikshuni used to look at herself in the mirror and adorn herself; another Bhikshu liked to climb trees and jump from one branch to another; still another always addressed others in a loud voice, with condescending terms and appellations.

In truth, however, all four had reached the stage of Arhatship. It is just that one of them was a buffalo in a previous life, another was a courtesan, another was a monkey, and still another belonged to the Brahman class. They were accustomed to these circumstances throughout many lifetimes, so that even when they had attained the fruits of Arhatship, their residual habits still lingered.

We also have the example of the Sixth Patriarch of Zen. Realising that the cultivators of his day were attached to a literal reading of the sutras and did not immediately recognise their Buddha Nature, he took the form of an ignorant and illiterate person selling wood in the marketplace. Or else, take the case of a famous Zen Master who, wishing to avoid external conditions and concentrate on his cultivation, took the expedient appearance of a ragged lunatic, raving and ranting. As a result, both distinguished Masters were criticised during their lifetimes. The Sixth Patriarch was faulted for his ignorance, while the Zen monk was called insane and berserk. Therefore, finding a good spiritual advisor is a difficult task indeed.

WAY OF COMPASSION

One day Siddhartha the future Buddha left Rajagrha to go to the foot of the mountain where many hermits and sages dwelt. On the way, he saw dust falling down from the mountain amidst the pounding sound of animal hoofs. Going closer, he found a large flock of sheep and goats moving along like a bank of clouds. They were being helplessly driven toward the city. At the rear of the flock, a little lamb was straggling, limping along painfully, its leg wounded and bleeding. Siddhartha noticed the little lamb and its mother walking in front of it constantly looking back in deep concern for her offspring. His heart was filled with pity. So Siddhartha took the little lamb with the wounded leg up into his arms, gently caressing it while walking along behind the flock.

When he saw the shepherds, he asked: 'Where are you driving this herd to? They should normally be driven back in the evening! Why do you drive them back at noontime?' The shepherds replied: 'The King is holding a big sacrifice today, and we have been ordered to bring one hundred sheep and goats each to the city at noontime.' Siddhartha said: 'I'll go with you.' He carried the little lamb in his arms all the way to the city. Walking behind the flock of sheep, Siddhartha reached the city; then he went toward the palace, where the sacrifice was being held.

The King and a group of priests of the fire-worshipping cult were chanting hymns, while a big fire was burning on the altar. They were about to kill the flock of sheep as a sacrifice, but when the leader of the fire-worshippers raised his sword to sever the head of the first sheep, Siddhartha quickly moved up and stopped him. In a grave and solemn manner, Siddhartha said to King Bimbisara: 'Your Majesty, don't let these worshippers destroy the lives of these poor animals.' Then he spoke to people who were standing as witnesses to this event: 'All living creatures cling to life. Why should people exert brutal force upon these friendly animals? The suffering of birth, old age, sickness and death will naturally take away their beloved lives.' Siddhartha continued: 'If human beings expect mercy, they ought to show mercy, for, according to the law of Cause and Effect, those who kill will, in turn, be killed. If we expect happiness in the future, we must do no harm to any kind of creature whatsoever. For whoever sows the seeds of sorrow and agony will undoubtedly reap the same fruits.' The manner in which Siddhartha spoke was peaceful and dignified and full of compassion yet, at the same, forceful and determined. He completely changed the intention and belief of the King and the fire-worshippers. So King Bimbisara asked Siddhartha to stay in his country to teach the people to be merciful. Siddhartha was deeply grateful, but since he had not yet attained his goal of Complete Enlightenment, he gracefully declined the invitation and departed.

Let's suppose that there is famine somewhere, a terrible famine of the kind that still happens in Africa. People are gaunt and emaciated, and there is terrible suffering.

In a certain town in the country which has been struck by this famine there live two men, one old, one young who each has an enormous quantity of grain, easily enough to feed all the people. The old man puts outside his front door a notice which reads:

'Whoever comes will be given food.' But after that statement there follows a long list of conditions and rules. If people want food they must come at a certain time, on the very minute. They must bring with them receptacles of a certain shape and size. And holding these receptacles in a certain way, they must ask the old man for food in certain set phrases which are to be spoken in anarchic language. Not many people see the notice, for the old man lives in an out-of-the-way street; and of those who do see it, a few come for food and receive it, but others are put off by the long list of rules. When the old man is asked why he imposes so many rules, he says 'That's how it was in my grandfather's time whenever there was a famine. What was good enough for him is certainly good enough for me. Who am I to change things?' He adds that if people really want food they will observe any number of rules to get it. If they won't observe the rules they can't really be hungry.

Meanwhile the young man takes a great sack of grain on his back and goes from door to door giving it out. As soon as one sack is empty, he rushes home for another one. In this way he gives out a great deal of grain all over the town. He gives it to anyone who asks. He's so keen to feed the people that he doesn't mind going into the poorest, darkest and dirtiest of hovels. He doesn't mind going to places where respectable people don't usually venture. The only thought in his head is that nobody should be allowed to starve. Some people say that he's a busybody, others that he takes too much on himself. Some people go so far as to say that he's interfering with the law of karma. Others complain that a lot of grain is being wasted, because people take more than they really need. The young man doesn't care about any of this. He says it's better that some grain is wasted than that anyone should starve to death.

One day the young man happens to pass by the old man's house. The old man is sitting outside peacefully smoking his pipe, because it isn't yet time to hand out grain. He says to the young man as he hurries past, 'You look tired. Why don't you take it easy?' The young man replies, rather breathlessly, 'I can't. There are still lots of people who haven't been fed.' The old man shakes his head wonderingly. 'Let them come to you! why should you go dashing off to them?' But the young man, impatient to be on his way, says 'They're too weak to come to me. They can't even walk. If I don't go to them they'll die.' 'That's too bad,' says the old man. 'They should have come earlier, when they were stronger. If they didn't think ahead that's their fault.'

But by this time the young man is out of earshot, already on his way home for another sack. The old man rises and pins another notice beside the first one. The notice reads: 'Rules for reading the rules.'

No doubt you've already guessed the meaning of the parable. The old man is the Arhat, representing Southern Buddhism, and the young man is the Bodhisattva, representing the Mahayana. The famine is the human

117

predicament, the people of the town are all living beings, and the grain is the Dharma, the teaching. Just as in principle both the old and the young man are willing to give out grain to everybody, so in principle both Southern Buddhism and the Mahayana are universal, meant for all. But in practice we find that the Theravada imposes certain conditions. To practice Buddhism within the Theravada tradition, even today, if you're taking it all seriously, you must leave home and become a monk or nun. You must live exactly as the monks and nuns lived in India in the Buddha's time. And you mustn't change anything. The Mahayana doesn't impose any such conditions. It makes the Dharma available to people as they are and where they are, because it is concerned solely with essentials. It's concerned with getting the grain to the people, not with any particular manner in which this is to be done. The Theravada expects people to come to it, so to speak, but the Mahayana goes out to them.

This difference between the Theravada and the Mahayana goes back to the early days of Buddhist history. About a hundred years after the Buddha's death, his disciples disagreed about certain issues so strongly that the spiritual community was split in two. Indeed, they disagreed about the very nature of Buddhism itself. One group of disciples held that Buddhism was simply what the Buddha had said. The Four Noble Truths, the Noble Eightfold Path, the Twelve Links or chain of conditioned co-production, the Four Foundations of Mindfulness — this was Buddhism. But the other group responded that this was not enough. Yes, all of these teachings did form part of Buddhism, but the example of the Buddha's life could not be ignored. The Buddha's teaching revealed his wisdom, but his life revealed his compassion, and both together made up Buddhism.

EVERYTHING IS MIND

There was once in China an expert archer. One day he went to a very high mountain with his bow on his back. While strolling on the mountain, he became thirsty and wanted some water to drink. Fortunately, he found a small spring under a bush, and he immediately bent over the water to drink it out of his hands until his thirst was quenched. However, when he finished drinking, he thought he saw a snake crawling in the water. He immediately felt sick and wanted to vomit the water he had drunk, but the water did not come out. He became seriously nervous about the water in his stomach, feeling something wriggling in it. When he got back home he became seriously ill. Numerous doctors gave him medical treatment, but in vain; finally, he became nothing but skin and bones, resigning himself to die.

One day a traveller stopped at his home. Seeing the condition of the patient, he asked the reason. The patient told him that he saw a snake crawling in the water of the spring and that he had swallowed the snake. The traveller said that he could cure the illness if the patient would do as he told him to do, taking him to the same spring where he had drunk the water.

He told the patient, who was bearing the same bow on his back, to take the same pose as he had before. The patient reluctantly bent over the water and was just going to scoop it up in his hands when he screamed out, that a snake was crawling in the water again. The man told him to be quiet and to observe the snake more closely. The archer got control of himself and found that it was not a snake at all, but the shadow of the bow he was carrying on his back.

The archer realised that the snake he thought he had swallowed before was only the shadow of his bow. After this, he felt quite relieved, and soon he regained his health.

We must recognise that our mind is the creator of our 'fate.' In this case, the dust of fear accumulated on the archer's mind. When he wiped off this dust, he become healthy again.

HUMAN REASONING

To approach the sutras 'making discriminations and nurturing attachments' is no different from the Zen allegory of a person attempting to lift a chair while seated on it. If he would only get off the chair, he could raise it easily. Similarly, the practitioner truly understands the Dharma only to the extent that he suspends the operation of the discriminating intellect, the faculty of the internal dialogue through which people from moment to moment define and perpetuate their customary world of perception.

SINGLE-MINDEDNESS

There was once a Zen monk meditating on a deserted mountain far away from all human habitation. Because of the rigors of the climate and the isolation of the place, he found it difficult to concentrate. His mind constantly wandered toward life in the village down below. One evening, as he was seated lost in errant thought, he had the sensation that he was being watched. He slowly turned his head, and lo and behold, there was a tiger crouched in the bushes behind him! One false move and the tiger would pounce on him. He had no choice but to remain ramrod straight, in single-minded concentration. When dawn broke, the tiger, fearful of the light of day, gave up this cat-and-mouse game and disappeared.

The next two evenings, the monk, faithful to his vow, resumed his meditation at the appointed time and place. The tiger returned and the scene repeated itself each evening. When daylight came on the third day, the monk, after three nights of singleminded concentration, experienced a Great Awakening, collapsed and died. At his funeral, a tiger was seen watching and wailing in the distance.

TRUTH
SUPARAGA AND THE POWER OF TRUTH

During one of his many lifetimes, the Buddha, as the sage
Suparaga, was a very wise ship captain. Even when he had
reached old age, he was known to be a lucky and fortunate
being.

Once, a group of sea traders, anxious for safe passage,
beseeched him to captain their ships. Suparaga replied to
them: 'I am an old man, how much assistance do you think I
can be? My mind wanders, my body is weak, and my
eyesight is almost gone.' But the merchants persisted: 'We
do not care about your physical condition, we do not want
you for your strength; we want you for your presence
alone.'

So, out of compassion, Suparaga, though old and
ailing, boarded the vessel — and they set off, with all the
merchants rejoicing.

Soon the ship lost sight of shore and found itself in the
realm of the Sea Serpents, that part of the great ocean
haunted by strange fish — a sea which churned with
surging waves buffeted by the whims of the screaming and
crying wind. Precious stones lay in the hidden depths where
nagas lived.

For days, the wind and sea ran high, and the vessel
moved with the current. No land came in sight and no
favourable sign came from the sea. The signs they did see
were strange to them, and the merchants grew increasingly
distraught, bedevilled by fear and despair. But Suparaga, the
Bodhisattva, comforted them saying: 'For those who would
cross the great ocean, such portentous turmoil is the rule.
Why wonder at it and fall prey to fear and emotionality?'

Before long, they found themselves approaching another sea, one shining with silver lustre, bright with a mass of white froth. The merchants said to Suparaga: 'What great sea is this, its waters veiled in foam like fine white linen? It seems covered with liquid moonbeams; it seems to show a laughing face.'

Suparaga said: 'This is difficult. We are driven too far. This is the sea called Milk Ocean. We should go no further. Turn back if you can!' But the merchants replied: 'The ship goes too quickly; the winds are too strong. It is impossible even to slow down, much less change course. The current drives us too swiftly and the winds blow contrary.'

Then having crossed that sea, they came to another, its rolling waves tinted with a golden splendour the colour of flames. Filled with amazement, the merchants said to Suparaga: 'Now the water appears like a huge, blazing fire! The waves are not blue, but seem tinged by the rising sun. What sea is this? Why is it this colour?'

Suparaga did not think it advisable to reveal the reason for the ocean's hue, but said only: 'The sea of Fire Garlands is its name. It would be wise indeed for us to turn back now.'

But they were unable to turn the ship, no matter how hard they struggled. And soon they were crossing into another sea, as green as the most brilliant emerald. The merchants said to Suparaga: 'Now the sea has yet another appearance. Its waters are the colour of emerald or aquamarine, and they shine like a beautiful meadow. What sea is this?'

Hearing this, Suparaga heaved a long and deep sigh, his heart aching with knowledge of the calamity that was imminent. In a low voice, he spoke: 'We have gone too far.

From here it will be hard to return. This is the Sea of Reeds at the end of the world.'

When they heard these words, the poor merchants were plunged into despair. Minds lethargic, limbs without power, they sat in dull apathy and did nothing but sigh.

After crossing that sea, in the afternoon near twilight, when the sun seemed to be setting into the ocean, a fearsome and tremendous noise arose. The ear-splitting sound struck fear into their hearts. It sounded like the sea rising in anger, like bamboo groves crackling with fire, like thunderclaps.

Suparaga, alarmed, cried out: 'Alas! Alas! You have come to the dreadful place from which no one returns, the Mare's Mouth, the mouth of the Lord of Death!'

At this, the poor merchants were stunned by the fear of death. Realising that all hope was lost, they wept, moaned and cried aloud to Suparaga: 'You, who have the ability to help all beings, who have so often relieved those in distress, now is the time to use your power for action. We take refuge in you, for we are sorely distressed and without any protection. The wrathful waters are about to swallow us like a morsel of food. The great Ocean will obey your command! Please put a stop to its terrible rage!'

Suparaga, his heart bursting with compassion, comforted the poor merchants, saying: 'I think I see a way to rescue us, but you must harness all your courage.'

Suparaga then threw his robe over one shoulder, knelt on the deck of the ship, and bowing down paid homage to the Tathagatas. Then he said: 'You, honourable sea traders, and you, sky and ocean-dwelling gods, listen and be my witness. Since my first conscious deed, I cannot recall even one instance of having injured any living being. By the power of this act of truth, by the strength of my store of virtuous actions, may this ship turn safely around without falling into the Mare's Mouth of death.'

And so great was the power of his truth, so great was the splendour of his merit, that the current and wind changed to the opposite direction, causing the vessel to return the way it came. And the ship, filled with the sound of her merry, laughing crew, her lovely white sails spread like wings, flew over the sea, a white swan in a pure and cloudless sky.

DRAGON KING'S SON

There was an old man named Ch'u. He was well over sixty. He had done many good things throughout his life. In the old days, transportation was very difficult. He donated money to have roads made and bridges built so people could get around more easily. People in need could always count on him for a handout. His neighbours had many good things to say about him. One day he saw a fisherman on his way to the market to sell a carp he had caught. This beautiful fish had red markings as bright and warm as a fire in the winter. Its eyes were as shiny as stars in the sky. Old Ch'u thought it would be a shame to eat such a beautiful fish, so he bought the carp for a good price and put it in a pond. He felt very good about that. But Ch'u was an old man, and nobody lives forever. Not long after that, he felt weak, giddy, and despondent. He thought he might not live much longer.

As he was lying home sick, a little servant boy came in, and said, 'Mister Ch'u, my master has sent me to invite you to eat with him.' Old Ch'u didn't recognise whose servant boy it was, but he thought getting out of bed might do him good; a meal out would lift his spirits. He followed the boy. 'I must really be sick,' he thought as they made their way, 'Everything looks hazy, and glowing in a golden light.' Before long, he found himself standing in front of an ornate palace with carved pillars and painted beams. A sign over the front door read, The Crystal Palace. 'Strange! Isn't that the name of the dragon's palace?' wondered Old Ch'u. In a few moments, out came his host, a most impressive man with thick eyebrows, long eye, and five long strands of whiskers. He looked lively and powerful, yet virtuous. After they had chatted a bit, Old Ch'u found out that his host was none other than the Dragon King himself! Together they enjoyed a rich feast of all the delicacies of mountain and sea. The Dragon King told Old Ch'u, 'One of my sons was out playing around the other day, and was kidnapped by a bandit who was going to murder him! Fortunately, you were there to save him. For this we are most grateful. 'Actually, your time on this earth is just about up, but because you have rescued a dragon in the guise of a fish, you have earned the right to live longer. I have prepared this simple repast to express my gratitude, and explain this to you.' 'I hardly dare to accept your generosity,' Old Ch'u humbly replied. 'From now on, I will do even more good deeds to show my deep gratitude.'

After their feast, Old Ch'u woke up in bed with a full stomach. 'It must have been a dream,' he told himself. 'But why am I so full?' He did many more good deeds, and died peacefully many years later without any suffering at the age of one hundred and twenty.